T0149249

HELP FROM
HEAVEN

OPENING THE WINDOWS

RANDAL A.
WIEDEMANN

WESTBOW
PRESS®
A DIVISION OF THOMAS NELSON
& ZONDERVAN

Copyright © 2016 Randal A. Wiedemann.

All rights reserved. No part of this book may be used or reproduced by any means, graphic, electronic, or mechanical, including photocopying, recording, taping or by any information storage retrieval system without the written permission of the author except in the case of brief quotations embodied in critical articles and reviews.

WestBow Press books may be ordered through booksellers or by contacting:

WestBow Press
A Division of Thomas Nelson & Zondervan
1663 Liberty Drive
Bloomington, IN 47403
www.westbowpress.com
1 (866) 928-1240

Because of the dynamic nature of the Internet, any web addresses or links contained in this book may have changed since publication and may no longer be valid. The views expressed in this work are solely those of the author and do not necessarily reflect the views of the publisher, and the publisher hereby disclaims any responsibility for them.

Any people depicted in stock imagery provided by Thinkstock are models, and such images are being used for illustrative purposes only.
Certain stock imagery © Thinkstock.

ISBN: 978-1-5127-2690-9 (sc)
ISBN: 978-1-5127-2691-6 (hc)
ISBN: 978-1-5127-2689-3 (e)

Library of Congress Control Number: 2016900133

Print information available on the last page.

WestBow Press rev. date: 2/12/2016

Contents

Bible References

New International Version (NIV) - Scripture taken from the HOLY BIBLE, NEW INTERNATIONAL VERSION®. Copyright © 1973, 1978, 1984 International Bible Society. Used by permission of Zondervan. All rights reserved. The "NIV" and "New International Version" trademarks are registered in the United States Patent and Trademark Office by International Bible Society. Use of either trademark requires the permission of International Bible Society. Bible references in this book are NIV unless otherwise noted.

Amplified Version (AMP) - Scripture taken from The Amplified Bible is used by permission of the Lockman Foundation and the Zondervan Corporation. Copyright © 1954, 1958, 1962, 1965, 1987 by the Lockman Foundation®. All rights reserved. Except as permitted under the U.S. Copyright Act of 1976, no part of this publication may be reproduced, distributed, or transmitted in any form or by any means, or stored in a database or retrieval system, without the prior permission of the publisher.

King James Version (KJV) - Authorized Version of the King James Bible. No copyright required.

The Holy Bible, New King James Version (NKJV) - Original work copyright © 1979, 1980, 1982 by Thomas Nelson, Inc. All rights reserved. Scripture from any of the Thomas Nelson translations may be quoted in any form (written, visual, electronic, or audio) up to two Hundred fifty (250) verses or less *without written permission*, as long as the Scripture does not make up more than 25 percent of the total text in the work and the Scripture is not being quoted in commentary or another Biblical reference work.

Foreword

For those of you disinterested in wading through a Foreword by some unknown person saying nice things about the author – allow me to cut to the chase: this book is grounded in one fundamental passion – restoring our broken relationship with our Father in Heaven. Although it covers the essentials of conviction, repentance, and salvation, this is a handbook for those who have truly committed their hearts to God and are asking, "Where do I go from here?" This is a practical step-by-step guide for restoring meaningful communications with our Creator – a relationship imbued with a love capable of moving mountains, and restoring true power and purpose in our lives.

You are now free to begin reading, "***Help from Heaven.***"

(For those of you who tend to read books sequentially in their entirety, seeking every savory morsel of information; or for those of you like me, who skipped the Foreword entirely, have already read most or all of the author's text, only to find that you now want to know more about him – the following is for you.)

I met Randal Wiedemann in the autumn of 1982. He was a young husband and father working as an aviation planner. I had recently completed college, and was striking out on whatever career and destiny God had waiting for me. For reasons that were not immediately evident, there was an instant connection between us that has grown exponentially over the span of three decades. Every passing year has drawn us closer as friends, business associates, and Christian brothers locked in a common mission.

During this time, I have known Randal as a man relentlessly hungry for truth, passionate for the things of God, and devoted to his family. He is a man of integrity... rare in today's world. He obediently served as the pastor of a church near Lexington, Kentucky. This led him to attend seminary in Cincinnati where he earned a Masters in Practical Ministries. At the same time, he was building a reputation for excellence as one of the top aviation consultants in America. In fact, the mission statement of his aviation consulting business is the single word, "Excellence," which says everything necessary about the man, his company, and his approach to life. His attention to detail and ability to excavate nuggets of truth often overlooked by others has fueled breakthroughs in both endeavors. These accumulated insights led to a calling to record them in book form.

Perhaps I should define what I mean by "a calling." We all know people who justify their own ambitions by sticking a sanctified sounding label on their efforts such as; *"I was led to write my life story"* or *"I was called to accomplish this exclusive endeavor."* All too often, that "call" or "leading" is little more than a desire for attention. As a pastor, I receive a regular flow of manuscripts by aspiring authors who believe they have a unique insight few – if any – have ever considered. It is the rare submission that manages to hold my attention for more than a third of the document. They generally fall into one of two very distinct categories; works of such remarkable simplicity, they permit only a brief wade and not a good swim; or works of such scholarly ambition, that even above average readers find them cumbersome and daunting. Jesus Christ, the Creator of the universe, spoke with profound simplicity. His words are direct, incredibly deep, and yet very accessible. I am all for simplicity, as long as there is significance. God does not intend for His Truth to be limited to scholars and theologians.

In the case of Randal Wiedemann, there have been numerous requests over the years from individuals sincerely urging him to record his spiritual insights in a format that could be recalled and shared. His writings began to be circulated in email format. Along the way, Randal developed a ministry as a pastor-to-pastors, speaking uncommon sense, truth, and encouragement to those on the front lines. We have been among those requesting him to gather his writings, instructions, and exhortations into book form.

The ultimate prompting however, occurred several years ago when Randal was chosen by a prophetically gifted brother at a Promise Keepers leader's prayer breakfast to receive a special anointing. Brother Rick was the leader of a men's prayer ministry and had been instructed by God to linger after the breakfast and see who the Spirit would reveal should receive a message, prayer, and an expensive ink pen. As it turned out, Randal was the individual selected. A conversation and prophetic prayer ensued in which Randal was encouraged to take up his pen and write what God was putting on his heart. These writings were to be published in book form. I suppose that we all need a stronger nudge from God at times, to get on to the next level.

Shortly following that encounter, Randal began to devote the earliest hours of his day – almost always before sunrise, and well before the phone started ringing – to seeking the Lord for guidance and inspiration. He recorded these conversations and awakenings in his first book, "*Five Minutes with Jesus.*" This wonderful work has become the second most requested title by the inmates served weekly by the Church Inside Out jail ministry. *(I'll give you one guess which "Book" is most requested).* These are men and women for whom traditional *church as usual* has failed to have a meaningful impact – before, during, and after their incarceration. These individuals have a highly attuned discernment for recognizing "phony." They crave what is "real." Once the Truth breaks through, they become hungry for all they can get. They have found Randal's words to be loaded with truth that effectively breaks down challenging spiritual concepts into easily applied insights.

I have no doubt that God can accomplish His good and perfect will in my life by any means He might choose. I am deeply thankful however, that one of His primary instruments has been the ministry and influence of Randal Wiedemann. I am certain that many lives have already been touched - and many more will be affected - by the words and ministry of this brother in Christ.

I am excited to get "*Help from Heaven*" into the hands of the spiritually hungry… to those genuinely seeking a real and meaningful relationship with our Creator. I am grateful for Randal's faithful service and partnership in the fulfillment of the Great Commission.

Rob Barber
Founding Pastor of the Church Inside Out
Outreach Minister of City Hill Ministry
Senior Evangelist of 321 Missions.

Preface

For full disclosure, I need to tell you I am a Christian. I did not come to Christianity simply because I was born into a Christian family. I came to Christ to survive. And yes, I did examine other religions - eastern mysticism, New Age, and other cults. But none gave me life except Christ. I have since gained complete respect for the Bible and its accuracy. It gives us a picture of heaven and hell and quotes Jesus on this subject.

I have found that many Christians are trying to do Christianity in their own strength, and it doesn't work. For some reason, we have missed crucial points that Jesus made about our faith and how it should be lived. By our own willing error, we have taken shortcuts that turned out wrong. Discouragement and depression have been the result. Unfortunately, we often find the harder we try to fix what's wrong, the worse off we get.

Without spoiling the punch line, this book is about receiving help from heaven in a way that removes obstacles from our path so we do not have to face them over and over. The help you receive can be instantaneous or it can take years. The time required depends on you. Heaven is ready right now and Christ has done all that is required to set you free from your trouble. However, your problem may have taken years to develop. Getting out of it, so that it doesn't return, may take some time too.

When Jesus prayed, "on earth as it is in heaven," He was giving us a solution to our problems. In heaven, there are no burdens as we know them. There are no personality disorders, no interrelationship problems or feuds, no disease, no sense of tragic sadness. Instead, heaven is the blueprint for perfection in every aspect of life on earth.

We know our children watch to see if we will do what we say we believe. But other people do the same thing – coworkers, extended family members, and church friends. Everyone is looking and learning. For this reason, thanks are due to my wife and family for overlooking my many faults as I write on this subject. They know the real me and how much I need the mercy and saving grace of Christ.

As you read this book, you will notice there are prayers throughout. I recommend you pray something like this beforehand: *Lord God, I desire to enter Your presence. Please open the eyes of my heart and let Your love and truth penetrate my mind, body, and spirit. May Your hand guide me and Your Spirit resonate within me as I read this book. Give me Your message and Your words. Thank You for Your help from heaven. Amen.*

Remember, while we may have temporary bouts with unhappiness, anyone living completely in Christ is joy-filled (Acts 13:52)!

Randal Wiedemann
May 2014

Help from Heaven

"Your kingdom come, Your will be done on earth as it is in heaven" (Mt 6:10). The prayer Jesus taught us calls for the establishment of God's kingdom and His will here on earth just as it is in heaven. So what is this heavenly kingdom that we are asking for and what do we know about it? There are people who say they have visited heaven for a short period of time. They may have been near death or "died" temporarily. During that time, most see a tunnel of light. At the end of the tunnel is a world of vibrant colors and sounds, with wonderful feelings of peace and love. Some recognize or speak with departed loved ones. Others talk about seeing Jesus there. But if they wrote these accounts, we can be sure the authors did not stay there. They received a glimpse and then came back to record what they saw in these heavenly visions.

These accounts notwithstanding, most of what we know about heaven comes from the Bible. The Bible describes the Holy City, Jerusalem, coming down out of heaven. The Holy City is bejeweled and has streets of translucent gold. It needs no sun or outside light because the whole place is brilliantly lighted with the refulgent glory of God. The Bible also describes the throne room of God and the worship offered by His living creatures there. Even with these descriptions, we know words cannot convey the holiness, majesty, awe, and brilliance of heaven. Words are only symbols representing a much greater reality.

Jesus taught His disciples about the kingdom of heaven, saying He had come down from heaven to do the will of God (Jn 6:38). By praying God's will be done "on earth as it is in heaven" we know heaven is a place where God's will is unhindered. It is a place of perfection.

"Nothing impure will ever enter it" (Rv 21:27a). The Bible says that in heaven, God "will wipe every tear from their eyes. There will be no more death or mourning or crying or pain, for the old order of things has passed away" (Rv 21:4). In short, heaven is a wonderful place with no sadness or dying. In heaven, the veil that covers our minds while we are on earth will be lifted, and a greater understanding and experience of God's love and peace will be given to us.

From these short descriptions, we understand that heaven is a place where all good things originate. Every problem that confronts us has its potential solution in the help available from our God in heaven. When Jesus performed miracles, He attributed them to God working within Him. All of the healing, the miraculous production of food, the giving of life to the dead - everything - came through Jesus from heaven. What's more, Jesus promised that His believers would participate in greater things than these because He was going to the Father in heaven (Jn 14:12). Do you need that type of help today? I certain do. As we walk together through the pages of this little book, let's explore how to better receive this help from heaven!

Part 1 – Preconditions

There is one major precondition to receiving constant and eternal help from heaven: a relationship with Jesus Christ. You may know of non-Christians who have had good fortune and answered prayers. Jesus said that God "causes His sun to rise on the evil and the good, and sends rain on the righteous and the unrighteous" (Mt 5:45). Life presents opportunities to the good and the bad. But that is not what I am talking about. I am talking about a direct path to God, which is not given to everyone. Jesus said, "I am the way and the truth and the life. No one comes to the Father except through me" (Jn 14:6). According to Jesus, the God of heaven is accessible only through Him.

What does "through Jesus" mean? It means dealing directly with Him in a personal way. There are many people sitting in church pews who agree with everything Jesus said, but they have never conducted any personal business with Him. If you asked these people about their relationship with Jesus, they would say something like "At church camp, I came forward when an altar call was made." Or "I've always been a Christian – I was born into the church and my parents brought me when I was young." Or "I prayed the sinner's prayer one night." They believe they have covered the precondition of faith in Jesus Christ. Only God knows whether or not a profession of faith is real and saving.

Jesus said, "Many will say to me on that day, 'Lord, Lord, did we not prophesy in your name, and in your name drive out demons and perform many miracles?' Then I will tell them plainly, 'I never knew you'" (Mt 7:22-23a). So there is no such thing as inherited Christianity. Authentic Christianity is marked by a genuine, live relationship with

Jesus Christ. We must do this first-hand and in person. A profession of faith may or may not be real, depending on whether a spiritual transaction has taken place (sometimes called "being born again"). How do you know whether or not this has really taken place? After all, many people pray for something and mean it.

Born Again

Until we are born again, we live in a closed system – a world within a world. We don't know about the larger world outside our bubble until it is pierced by God. Talking with people who have been through a born-again experience, there are a number of consistent descriptions of what happens. These include:

- A clear moment of being born again. There is a before and after.
- A change on the inside, where forgiveness of sin is actually realized. Typically, a spiritual weight is lifted from the person.
- An inner desire to follow God and learn to obey Him.
- A new sense of being loved by God. This is something that cannot be taken away.

Through this process, we are touched by God. Many gain a deeper understanding of Jesus and confirmation that He is who He said He is. When we are born again, we are regenerated in our hearts with a righteousness that is not our own. And we know it is not from ourselves. It is an alien righteousness - the righteousness of Christ. No wonder it feels so different and so good!

I realize that feelings are different in each person. They are subjective. So people will not all feel the same thing when they are born again. But one thing should be clear; there is a definite change after the new spiritual birth. How that change manifests in different people is between them and Christ.

Our connection with God through the Holy Spirit has baffled "un-born-again" people for centuries and has created deep divisions in the Church. Can you see why the born-again process has been so misunderstood? It is the spiritual implantation of Christ in our hearts so He can do good works *through* us. When we are born again, it is a distinct occurrence, where we transact directly with God. The Holy Spirit living inside us is not a metaphor or a poetic way of claiming God's stamp of approval. It is real and experiential. If you have it, you know it. If you don't have it, don't tell everyone that it isn't possible or that it's some spiritual mumbo-jumbo. Instead, seek God diligently for it and He will fill you with Himself if you don't quit or give up.

For me, it was surrender, followed by a touch from God in the planting of new life in my body. Joyce Meyer, the evangelist, said that it was like being unzipped and having living love poured into her body and then being zipped back up. It took about three weeks for that incredible glow to dissipate. No matter how we experience it, being born again is a touch from God that changes everything. But even if it feels different, it is the same multifaceted Holy Spirit that lives within each Christian.

If you do not think you have been born again, let us pray: *Lord Jesus, I know in my mind that You are who You say You are. I have asked You to forgive all of my sins in the past, but somehow, we haven't connected on a level that has been life-changing for me. I know that with Your touch I will never be the same. So I repent of the sins You bring to mind right now. I ask for Your complete forgiveness and I surrender my life to You. I really do. Show me what it is to be truly born again of Your Spirit. I thank You and ask this in Your Name. Amen.*

Being born again won't automatically fix all of our problems. Our relationship with Jesus is not a one-and-done event. It is a *living* process. It takes time and help from heaven to get through problems. In fact, problems are gifts from God that get us to communicate with Him more frequently. After having endured many of the problems listed in this book, I can share insights that may speed up your help from heaven. We are often blind to a number of issues that should be resolved simply by knowing Jesus. But it sometimes takes a "coach" to help us through. I certainly had a number of very good Christian mentors who helped me.

Cleansing from Jesus

Jesus said, "Be perfect, therefore, as your heavenly Father is perfect" (Mt 5:48). There is no reason to argue about it or deny that God would require perfection from us. When Jesus gave the Sermon on the Mount

(Mt 5-7), He said if we even think evil thoughts, we have broken the law of God. For example, if a man looks at a married woman with lust, he has committed adultery with her. If someone hates someone else, they have murdered that person in his or her mind. Do you see the standard Jesus set is perfection?

By our own thoughts we are guilty of sin and subject to God's punishment. If we believe we deserve anything good from God for our actions, we either have a higher estimate of the purity and goodness of our actions than really exists or we have underestimated God's perfect standards for behavior. These standards make it impossible to keep God's moral laws in our own strength. And that is why we must have Jesus to help us.

The Good News, or the Gospel, involves the atonement of Jesus Christ for our sins. For many years, I had the wrong idea of what it meant to have Jesus forgive my sins. I thought the price Jesus paid on the cross for my sins took those sins away as if they had never happened. I thought I wouldn't have to deal with them at all after asking Jesus to forgive me. Unfortunately, the guilt from a number of these sins came back to haunt me - as if they had not been forgiven.

I learned from the Bible that Jesus is a "propitiation" or payment for our sins. "And he is the propitiation for our sins: and not for ours only, but also for the sins of the whole world" (1 Jn 2:2 KJV). *Propitiation* means an atoning sacrifice. Jesus is the Redeemer who paid for our sins with His life. "In him we have redemption through his blood, the forgiveness of sins" (Eph 1:7).

If we think about this as a trial in which Satan is the prosecutor and Jesus is the defense attorney, God is the righteous judge who will render a just decision about our sins. In my previous way of thinking, I was hoping my sins would stay quiet and never go to trial. I wanted to "settle out of court" and hide them to protect my reputation. I thought because Jesus had forgiven me, none of that messy process would have to be endured. It was like being guilty but never getting caught. I thought if I was justified by Jesus, it meant "just-if-I'd" never sinned. But that is not entirely true.

4

The Bible asserts that my trial *is* held and that I *am* found guilty of my sins. This is completely within the realm of justice and reality. I did commit the sins, and so I am guilty. I cannot remain secretive or in denial about my sins. However, when God pronounces the sentence of death for these sins, Jesus takes that punishment for me through faith. This doesn't change the fact that I am guilty, but it does resolve the legal issues and punishment surrounding my guilt. My debt to society (as they used to call the punishment of criminals) has been paid. I am a free man, not because I wasn't caught but because Jesus paid my penalty.

Now, my attitude is different from when I was in denial of my sin through the convenient "magic" of Jesus. Before, I simply ran away in shame from owning up to my sin. I thought if Jesus could erase it from ever happening, I could turn a blind eye toward my former wrongdoing. This view of forgiveness can actually encourage more sin and is sometimes called "cheap grace."

But after realizing the full price of forgiveness and justice, I now must fully repent before God and ask in faith for the atoning grace of Jesus to cover my sins. By owning up to my specific sins, I am able to repent of them and receive forgiveness. I can look at the Judge and not hang my head - I am square with all that justice demands. That cannot happen while I am in denial, scared to confess, or hiding my sins. This is why we must repent of our sins by name. We cannot be vague about it.

Once I have been exonerated in the sight of God, I have a humble spirit and complete thankfulness. I realize what it cost Jesus to pay for my sins - death upon the cross! There is no double jeopardy for those sins. I cannot be re-tried once Jesus has taken my punishment. I can live in joy because the legal barrier of my sin keeping me away from God is removed and I am in fellowship with Him.

Let us pray: *Dear Lord Jesus, thank You for redeeming me from my sin and empowering me to live for You. Help me to enter Your presence daily and wait on You in the inner chamber of my heart. May the truth and freedom that You have given me be infectious to other people, setting them free as well. May Your joy be complete as I spread Your Word to all of those in my circle of influence, for I ask this in Your name. Amen.*

The Way It Is Supposed to Work

If you attend a church regularly and partake of its sacraments and are not being conformed inwardly to Christ-likeness, then your religion is like that of the Pharisees. True Christianity remakes us on the inside because the Holy Spirit of Christ lives there. The mystical union we have with Christ when we are born again in the Spirit reflects the words of Jesus when He said, "I pray also for those who will believe in me through their message, that all of them may be one, Father, just as you are in me and I am in you. *May they also be in us* so that the world may believe that you have sent me. I have given them the glory that you gave me, that they may be one as we are one: *I in them and you in me.* May they be brought to complete unity to let the world know that you sent me and have loved them even as you have loved me" (Jn 17:20-23, emphasis added).

Jesus made it clear on the night before His crucifixion that the Holy Spirit is to live inside us. From there, it is He doing good works through us. We are not subcontractors to Him, working good deeds and then taking the results to Him for reward. No. Jesus talked about how it worked between Him and the Father: "Don't you believe that I am in the Father, and that the Father is in me? The words I say to you are not just my own. Rather, it is the Father, living in me, who is doing his work. Believe me when I say that I am in the Father and the Father is in me; or at least believe on the evidence of the miracles themselves" (Jn 14:10-11).

Jesus used other analogies for His disciples. In John 15, Jesus said that He is the Vine and they are the branches. "Remain in me, and I will remain in you. No branch can bear fruit by itself; it must remain in the vine. Neither can you bear fruit unless you remain in me" (Jn 15:4). This helps to clarify what it means to have Jesus living in us and we in Him. Our inner strength comes from life-giving sap of the Vine. We cannot produce fruit without Him.

What is fruit in this case? It is good works, refreshment, and spiritual food for others that actually benefits them. "I am the vine; you are the branches. If a man remains in me and I in him, he will bear much fruit; apart from me you can do nothing" (Jn 15:5). Jesus was telling us that He must live in us. There is a spiritual "transplantation" that happens when we are born again. Without Jesus, we simply go through the mechanized motions and ultimately are cut off from life itself. However, with Jesus, we have a root system that extends through the Vine, drawing life down from heaven.

Let us pray: *Lord Jesus, I ask Your Holy Spirit to live in me and through me. If I haven't transacted personally with You in the past, may that happen now. Please help me overcome any obstacles to this union. I believe You are who You say You are. I thank You and ask this in Your name, Amen.*

Why Jesus?

Americans believe in pluralism. There are numerous political parties. There are many different religions. This is the American way! But Jesus insisted that the *only* way to God was through Him (Jn 14:6). He said that no one (this is a universal negative, meaning *not anyone*) comes to the Father except through Jesus. How can Jesus insist on just one path to heaven? Why didn't God provide many paths? And isn't it overly simplistic to reduce the truth or falseness of a religion to this litmus test? Not according to Jesus.

The Bible says about Jesus, "In the beginning was the Word, and the Word was with God, and the Word was God. He was with God in the beginning. Through him all things were made; without him nothing was made that has been made" (Jn 1:1-3). This statement is saying Jesus is God incarnate and the second Person of the Godhead.

If Jesus is not God, then His exclusive claims are not valid. However, if God were to say no one could come to Him except through Jesus, then it is the utmost arrogance to deny that statement and substitute our own made-up path to heaven. So if Jesus is God, then what He says is absolute law. We are not being humble by inventing many paths to heaven or writing Jesus out of His role of cosmic government.

In short, the question as to "why Jesus?" is answered, "because He said so." It was Jesus (not His followers) who laid down the conditions for coming to Him and to God the Father. Countless Christians throughout the ages have found this to be experientially true.

Surrender to Jesus

Jesus said, "No one can come to me unless the Father has enabled him" (Jn 6:65). So let's review the bidding. Jesus is saying no one can come to Him unless the Father has drawn him or her. Jesus also says no one can come to the Father except through Him. At first glance, this seems to be a circular reference. But a closer look shows that God orchestrates our salvation through the divine Gate of Jesus. This is the key! Unless your heart is inclined to Jesus, the Father has not enabled you. Surrender to Jesus is the last thing we voluntarily want to do unless there is supernatural inclination in our hearts. We may want the benefits of a relationship with Jesus, such as love and inner peace, but we will not want Jesus Himself unless our hearts have been made ready.

So who controls our inclinations? When Jesus says no one can come to Him unless the Father has enabled him, it sounds as if God is in control of our desire to come to Jesus. Without getting into the deep subject of the freedom of the human will, let's simply leave it where Jesus left it. Unless God does something to our inner desires, we don't want to come to Jesus on our own. That is, we can't want something we don't actually want. We can pretend we want it and most people won't know we're pretending. But we know! And God knows! This is why faith is such a personal matter. Ultimately, it is only between God and us.

Most of us need to get to the end of our own resources and efforts before we will consider help from heaven. Inwardly, we know we need Him, but we also know what we will have to give up in order to have Him. The punch line in the story of Jesus and the rich young ruler comes to mind here. "When Jesus heard this, he said to him, 'You still lack one thing. Sell everything you have and give to the poor, and you will have treasure in heaven. Then come, follow me.' When he heard this, he became very sad, because he was a man of great wealth" (Lk 18:22-23). Have you weighed what it will cost to surrender to Jesus? Must God make your situation so desperate you don't value the material things of this world? What about your reputation, your pride, or your health?

God will not ask us to do something that He has not already granted us the power to do. He supplies the courage. He supplies the healing. He supplies the inner power to overcome our desire to justify our sin to a holy God. "For it is God who works in you to will and to act according to his good purpose" (Phil 2:13). We need not act alone. We cannot act alone. God must work in us through His Holy Spirit so that we can act according to His good purpose. Our job is to believe that He will supply all that is needed.

Let us pray: *Dear Lord Jesus, I have tried and failed to live a life free of sin. The harder I try, the worse it gets. I realize that I cannot do this alone. I now surrender to You and ask You to do in me whatever is pleasing in Your eyes. Help me to experience Your love in a real way. May Your love guide me and instill in me the power to live in Your strength. I trust You to keep me from returning to my old sinful ways. I ask this in Your name, Amen.*

Surrender and Obedience

Surrender to Jesus is tied directly to our willingness to obey Him. What we are surrendering is our right to run our own lives. Because of the strong nature of our carnal minds, it is impossible to single-handedly come to a "decision" for Christ. God must enable us to do this by melting our hearts with His love. We can experience this love more fully as we spend time waiting in the presence of God.[1]

This is not an easy issue. Our own obstinacy is so ingrained we don't often know when we are hearing Christ or simply listening to the desires of self. We must ultimately come to the point of not trying to justify *in our own minds* actions we have undertaken without Christ. The mercy and forgiveness of Christ is our only justification and righteousness. You may want to repeat the following affirmation and let it sink into your thoughts: *"I surrender to You, Lord Jesus, and ask that Your Holy Spirit live through me to think, act, do, and feel the way You would. I believe and obey You every day in every way with reverence."*

This doesn't guarantee obedience to Christ, but it does permit us to think about and dwell on the various aspects of obedience to Him. Our minds should be steeped in readiness to obey Christ's commands and bathed in His presence. Even if we don't feel His presence when we

---

[1] I recommend *The Practice of the Presence of God* by Brother Lawrence. It is a short read, but very valuable to your spiritual journey.

make these affirmations, we can be assured He hears us and is working to give us the ability to obey Him and get closer to Him.

Where Is Real Power and Security?

The best thing about surrendering to Jesus is that we experience the source of real power and security. For many years, I was confused about these things. When I was young, I thought the boxer, Cassius Clay, – who later became Mohamed Ali – exemplified the powerful person. He made claims about defeating his opponents and then did it. He wasn't bragging because he backed it up. It was like Babe Ruth pointing to the outfield with his bat and then hitting a homerun in that direction. I admired and wanted self-assured power because I believed it would protect me and give me security.

The older I get, the more I realize real power is located in the person who controls my destiny. When King David committed adultery with Bathsheba and had Uriah killed, his prayer for forgiveness was directed at God: "Against you, you only, have I sinned and done what is evil in your sight" (Ps 51:4). *You only?* What about Uriah and Bathsheba? Didn't David sin against them? I suppose so. But David knew the ultimate penalty for his sin rested with God, and as such, He was the only source of forgiveness.

Let me stress this, if people can forgive me and keep me from eternal penalty, then *they* have real power over me. If God alone can do that, *He* has real power over me. Jesus said, "But I will show you whom you should fear: Fear him who, after the killing of the body, has power to throw you into hell. Yes, I tell you, fear him" (Lk 12:5). It is not the devil to whom Jesus is referring. Jesus is speaking about God who exercises this authority

Until we acknowledge that God alone controls our destiny, we will live in unbelief, where we give power and authority to secondary causes which cannot save us. The first Commandment is to have no other gods before the one true God. Even misidentifying the power of God and His authority is a form of idolatry. It may sound narrow minded, but our security rests only in the One who saves us.

Let us pray: *Lord Jesus, may I know beyond any shadow of doubt that You are the Source of all power and security. I repent for giving power and authority to idols in my heart. May I go to You first rather than work my plan and then pray later for Your help with it. Unless You build my life, my efforts are in vain. I pray this in Your holy name, Amen.*

What We All Know

Before I was reborn in the Spirit, I used to have a recurring nightmare. In my dream, I was in school and the end of the term had arrived. It was the night before final exams and I would remember there was an early morning class that I had stopped attending sometime back near the beginning of the semester. I simply forgot about this class until the night before the final. When I remembered that I had to take the exam, I would try to get notes from other students, cram for the exam, and worry about failure. I would wake up in a cold sweat, having a terrible feeling about forgetting something very important. Back then, when I realized it was just a dream, I would pass it off as a nightmare. After I surrendered to the Lord, I was given the real meaning of the dream.

The class I was skipping was the spiritual side of my life. I had "signed up" for this class at the beginning of my life and then dropped out. I remember, as a young boy, being fascinated with butterflies, dinosaurs, rock collections, stars and galaxies, and all of the wonder of the created world. I remember not being afraid to go to God and enjoy His presence. That wonder slowly died as my world became busy with secular and then profane pursuits. Eventually, my preoccupation with the world and my engagement with sin focused my thoughts on myself. I forgot about my heavenly school with God and no longer spent time with Him.

How about you? Does that sound familiar? The Final Exam is that moment when we must stand alone before God and give an account of our lives. I had no excuse for skipping His class. I had become afraid to take risks for God and had not completed the course requirements. I had quit this part of my life, and over time, God no longer seemed familiar. Failure would mean consignment to hell. It was truly a nightmare I wanted to forget.

And that is just the point. We all, Christians and non-Christians, have a knowledge of God given to us from birth. The Bible says we universally suppress and intentionally forget that knowledge in order to live as we please. When people are reminded of this, they either agree and repent, or they react violently against the person or institution that spoke this truth.

R.C. Sproul taught that we are not to be one of those people who at the Day of Judgment says, "God, I didn't know the gun was loaded! If I had only known what You wanted, I would have been one of your greatest supporters. But You didn't make it clear to me what I was supposed to do when I was alive." The fact is, we do know. Deep in our hearts, we are perfectly aware of who God is and the difference between right and wrong.

Let us pray: *Lord Jesus, please reawaken me to the knowledge of You that was placed in me at birth. Open my heart and mind that I may truly share with You everything in my life. May You lead and guide me into obedience and loving friendship with You now and forever. Amen.*

Sowing and Reaping

In bringing Part 1 to a close, there is one foundational precept you already know. That is, to better receive help from heaven, we must acknowledge the principle of sowing and reaping. It is a Christian principle; but it is recognized more broadly with names like karma, investment, the "Golden Rule," paying dues, just rewards, payback, etc. People know it works. The Bible says, "Do not be deceived: God cannot be mocked. A man reaps what he sows" (Gal 6:7). If we are to reap rewards from heaven, we will have to sow seeds of the Spirit.

For material rewards, the same principles apply. There is a challenge from God to all of us in Malachi 3:10: "'Bring all the tithes into the storehouse, that there may be food in My house, and try Me now in this,' says the Lord of hosts, 'If I will not open for you the windows of heaven and pour out for you such blessing that there will not be room enough to receive it'" (NKJV). God says, "Try me in this" which means *test* Me in this. That is an open challenge to you and me. Have you ever experimented with giving? I have, and I found that we cannot out-give

God. He works through the principle of sowing and reaping so much so that we could call it a natural law.

This principle has incredible implications about how to receive help from heaven. God has already set up mechanisms that will naturally provide this help. If we sow the seed of generosity, we will receive generously. If we sow negative things, well, you can guess what happens. Unfortunately, most of us are reaping negative rewards from our actions. We need intervention from heaven to stop the bad consequences and to give us a new start. If you are having this trouble, take heart. This book teaches methods to interrupt negative cycles of sowing and reaping through the grace of Jesus Christ.

Let us pray: *Almighty God, thank You for sending Jesus to pay the price of my sin to relieve me of guilt. I ask You now to forgive my foolish and sinful sowing so I may not reap the resulting harvest. Instead, I ask for Your mercy and grace to reawaken the spiritual adventure You planned for me before I was born. For so long I have only considered myself and my personal needs. Your love is changing my cold heart and opening my world to You and Your radiant presence. Please help me to live each day in loving communication and obedience to You. I ask this in Jesus' name, Amen.*

Part 2 - Looking Inward

In seeking help from heaven, we need to correctly identify who we are and who God is. Many people, including Christians, get this wrong. So let's first take an inventory of our motives. If our motives are right, God will reward us. But we are warned: "When you ask, you do not receive, because you ask with wrong motives, that you may spend what you get on your pleasures" (Jas 4:3). God is being gracious to us if He withholds things that will hurt us or that we will waste on our selfish pleasures.

Two Different People

When we delve into motives, it gets complicated because most of us function as two different people – the person we project on the outside and the person we really are on the inside. Often the two do not match. We have learned that to get along with people, we often have to mask our true motives, which may make us look selfish, uncaring, or politically incorrect. We often say or do things calculated to get the response we want.

Jesus called the Pharisees and Scribes hypocrites or "pretenders" because they showed one type of pious behavior to the world while on the inside they were selfish and wicked. Jesus reserved some of His harshest criticism for this lack of integrity. On the other hand, I believe that Jesus got along with the tax collectors and prostitutes because they were the same on the outside as they were on the inside. Jesus could work with that type of transparent and consistent behavior even if it was wrong.

The greater the deception about our inner identity and motives, the more defiled and corrupt a person we will be. Jesus wants us to be completely honest, not just with Him, but with ourselves. The inside person must match the person we project on the outside. A side benefit of this honesty is that it positions us to receive true help from heaven when we need it.

In Jesus' parable about the prodigal son, we find redemption and healing that begins with complete honesty. If you remember the story, the prodigal son left home with his inheritance, which he spent in drunkenness and debauchery. Before he could be healed, he first had to acknowledge and agree with his true position. The Bible says "he came to himself."

How could he not already be himself? Only if he was living a dual life. This parable captures the split between the inner and outer person. We will never be happy in our relationship with God or with people until who we are on the inside matches the person on the outside. So as long as we are functioning as two different people, heaven's help would only compound our split-personality behavior. The Bible warns us if we are "double-minded" we cannot expect to receive anything from the Lord (Jas 1:7-8).

Healing of the prodigal son's schism began when he faced the truth that he was a sinner and a failure - by his own actions. Without God or hope of redemption, people in his position often blame other people or even commit suicide. But the good news God has for us is that there is always hope of a new beginning. And it starts with complete honesty.

Let us pray: *Lord Jesus, please help me with my lack of integrity. I want to be the same person on the inside as on the outside. If I am not who I should be, please help me be honest and seek You to fix the split within myself. May You draw me into oneness with Yourself and the Father. I ask this in Your holy name. Amen.*

My Surrender

The story of the Prodigal Son is my story. It resonates with me because it describes my conversion experience. Back in the mid-1970s, I was living as two people. My life had spun out of control with the use of alcohol, the mindless pursuit of women, and a deep sense of emptiness. Yet, I could still go to work and act as if I had it together. But over time, I felt my internal energy and resources were running out. Keeping up appearances was hard work.

Finally, it became impossible to pretend everything was okay. I was playing with the tools of death and was somehow magnetically attracted to them. I was in real trouble. Yet there was no pill, no shot, or no medicine that could heal me. The sickness was in my mind and soul. I began to recognize my own depravity and wondered how I could ever experience the joy of purity again. I had become completely cynical and I could not unscramble that egg. I needed a fresh start, but I didn't know of any "reset button." With all of my fleshly sins and my darkened mind, how in the world could I simply ditch those and start new? My guilt was chained to me and I couldn't escape.

I thought about going to church; but to explain my situation to a clergyman would not absolve me of my guilt. That man of God, no matter how holy, did not have the power to unchain me from my sins. Seeking help from other people might have resulted in the public exposure of the depraved person I was on the inside and I didn't want to face that shame. I slowly began to realize that no human being could fix me. It finally dawned on me that God was the answer.

My help had to come from heaven. However, this presented a problem. I was not on speaking terms with God and wasn't sure what I would have to do to gain an audience with Him. When I thought about going before Him, I became terrified on the inside. The mere thought of a just and holy God looking at my sinful life scared me to the core. I couldn't face Him! My fear was too great. And worse - I knew that I was responsible for my situation.

I began to worry about the penalty for my sins. And so I did what most people do in this situation: I tried to escape from God and from being alone with my thoughts. I would escape by keeping busy, getting drunk, hanging out with friends, watching TV - doing anything rather than face the reality of my condition.

Finally, the day came in November of 1975 I knew I must stop running from God and surrender to Him. I don't know how I knew, except I sensed an internal ultimatum: surrender or die. I wasn't sure if God would punish me or take my life upon my surrender, but I had run out of rebellious energy and could not flee from God's tribunal of justice any longer. It occurred to me at the time that if the universe was evil, with only death and destruction waiting for everyone who ever lived, then having this evil deity kill me would actually be doing me a favor.

That evening, as I prepared for possible death or personal annihilation, I readied myself for surrender to God. I felt as though I was on death row on the day of execution. I knew my surrender must be unconditional and that I would have to bare my hidden inner self to God and let Him deal with my defiled mind and soul. Whatever His punishment was to be, it was deserved. My fear of the unknown was off the charts. But I knew I had come to the end of my escape route.

The Moment of Surrender

People in the Bible who come into actual contact with God for the first time have similar reactions - they fall apart. The Israelites did it at Mount Moriah. Isaiah did it when he was called as a prophet. The shepherds did it in Bethlehem. Even the disciples did it when the glory of Jesus was revealed. Most of us have shields that keep us from being burned up by the brilliant light of God. But there are times when the shield is lifted. That is when the fear of holiness grips us.

I had a dreadful fear of holiness in my apartment that night. Even so, I released my iron grip on my soul and surrendered to God, thinking that He would kill me. To my complete surprise, God accepted me! Instead of striking me dead, He instantly surrounded me with love and acceptance. I was the prodigal son who had rehearsed his confessional speech, only to be embraced in the loving arms of my heavenly Father. For me, there was an actual tangible transaction with heaven that I felt physically, mentally, emotionally, and spiritually. I had moved from death to life.

God caught me in His arms as I let go from my precarious perch in my own dark world. He began a healing process in my mind and soul that night, removing the guilt and torment that had beleaguered me. I had been born again in the Spirit. But I had only just begun my journey. It took years and years of living out what He had put in me that night to get to where I can even write about this and attempt to explain it to you.

I am not against medicine, counseling, clergy, or doctors in general. They are all helpful and needed. However, when the problem is our pride and the denial of our own darkened souls, we need to face facts honestly. Not only is God the only source of life, but He is also the only source for remission of our sins and guilt. Our friends can't resolve our sin problems. Neither can we be relieved of true guilt by prescribed medicine nor talks with a psychologist. But until we actually surrender our darkened hearts to Jesus, we will try desperately to find another way.

Let us pray: *Lord Jesus, I come to You in surrender again. Somehow, the world has crept back into my soul. I need You. Please cleanse me from sin and help me to live in Your Spirit. Please give me the authentic desire to love and serve You for the rest of my life. Thank You for hearing my prayer. Amen.*

Singleness of Mind and Heart

After I first came to the Lord in surrender, it took about four months of constantly seeking Him before the fullness of God's peace descended upon me. Now, I believe God designed the timing and process of my experience specifically for me because of my personality. Your situation will be different. But that doesn't change the principles involved. The fullness of God's peace comes, in part, through the single-mindedness of seeking Him.

The followers of Jesus in the Upper Room demonstrated single-mindedness when the Holy Spirit descended upon them. It occurred after Jesus ascended into heaven right before their eyes. After that happened, the Bible says, "Then they returned to Jerusalem from the hill called the Mount of Olives, a Sabbath day's walk from the city. When they arrived, they went upstairs to the room where they were staying. Those present were Peter, John, James and Andrew; Philip and Thomas, Bartholomew and Matthew; James son of Alphaeus and Simon the Zealot, and Judas son of James. They all joined together constantly in prayer, along with the women and Mary the mother of Jesus, and with his brothers" (Acts 1:12-14).

So the disciples and others went upstairs and began praying. They were not going to stop until they had an answer from heaven. After 10 days of constant prayer, something happened: "When the day of Pentecost came, they were all together in one place. Suddenly a sound like the blowing of a violent wind came from heaven and filled the whole house where they were sitting. They saw what seemed to be tongues of fire that separated and came to rest on each of them. All of them were filled with the Holy Spirit and began to speak in other tongues as the Spirit enabled them" (Acts 2:1-4). In other words, God touched them directly with His Holy Spirit.

If we are determined and will not quit, then anything that stands in our way can be surrendered and placed on the altar of our hearts to be given up to God. In my own healing, I came to the point of declaring to myself over and over, "I will never quit, I will never give up." Just saying that to myself gave me strength to get through the next hour. The thought here is that if I believe God will come and I hold out long enough, God indeed will rescue me. God wants us to be determined! Truly, if you will never quit, God will respond to you with help from heaven.

Let us pray: *Lord Jesus, I pray for singleness of mind and heart. Help me to be determined to come into Your presence. I believe You when You said that any who come to You would not be driven away. Bid me to come to You, Lord, and fill me with Your glorious presence. I ask this in Your name, Amen.*

What If I Still Have Remorse Over My Sinful Past?

Many new Christians have some remorse over their lives from before they became a new creation. A certain amount of this is healthy, keeping us from returning to our former sinful ways. But if it becomes an obsession or a nagging set of doubts as to our purification from sin, it can actually hurt our witness as new creatures in Christ.

You and I have an enemy. That enemy is called "the accuser" of our brothers (Rv 12:10). The devil's job is to bring up our past sins and rub them in our faces. It is then we must fight this guilt with our faith in God's promises of cleansing and renewal, spelled out in His Word. If ever there were a time we needed a high view of Scripture, now is that time. We need to believe the Bible is absolutely God's Word and that it conveys His authority. Otherwise, we have nothing to fight the enemy's accusation of our guilt except our feelings. As you and I know, feelings change from day to day.

In our own minds and hearts, we need to affirm that we are on God's side and that we believe in His justification and purification of our souls to *His satisfaction*. When the Bible says: "If we confess our sins, he is faithful and just and will forgive us our sins and purify us from all unrighteousness" (1 Jn 1:9), we must believe it completely. Further, we must also forgive ourselves for those sins, because we are not more righteous than God. He is our only hope against the bitter remembrance of past sins.

God has done everything necessary to clear us of *all* wrongdoing. We need to believe in His promise of cleansing to the uttermost by the blood of Jesus. "But if we walk in the light, as he is in the light, we have fellowship with one another, and the blood of Jesus, his Son, purifies us from *all* sin" (1 Jn 1:7, emphasis added).

"But what if I continue to sin or am tempted to sin, even after my conversion?" When that happens to me, I feel doubly ashamed. After all, I'm writing a book about this. So I have to take my own advice I got from the Bible. But here's a secret the enemy doesn't want you to know - everyone sins after conversion! Does that make it right? Of course not! But Jesus knew exactly what He was getting when He saved you and me. He knows our shortcomings. He knows our future sins.

Jesus has a great victory planned for all who never quit or give up believing He will cleanse them from sin. Even when we sin and think of Him during the sin, and how ashamed we are of it, He is working. The very remembrance of Him is proof He has not forgotten us and left us to our own devices. He will save us absolutely and completely because He has declared it in His Word.

If we continually seek to enter His presence, we will eventually begin to experience the joy of His companionship that outshines any temptation to sin. He will align our desires such that we simply will not *want* to do whatever seems to have sinful power over us. This may take a long time or it could happen overnight. But He breaks our bondage by giving us a hunger and desire for righteousness and to be in loving fellowship with Him. We overcome evil with good.

So do not be worried that you are not moving quickly enough into the super-Christian mold. Our idea of what God is after and His idea are two different visions. He is working within you and me right now. Even if you feel weak and unable to act on your convictions, your most important job is to believe that Jesus is able to be your strength in this area. This is faith. This is the path of help from heaven for all of us. Our sin is only for a season and we can use it to remind ourselves of our total dependence on Jesus to win the battle for our minds and hearts.

Let us pray: *Lord Jesus, sometimes I catch myself dredging up the memory of old sins that You have previously forgiven. I am attempting to clean my slate and justify myself without You during these times. Please forgive me for trying to earn righteousness. I do believe Your Word about the complete forgiveness and redemption of my sin. Thank You for reminding me. Amen*

Focus on Now and the Future

The apostle Paul had this inner desire: "Brothers and sisters, I do not consider myself yet to have taken hold of it. But one thing I do: Forgetting what is behind and straining toward what is ahead, I press on toward the goal to win the prize for which God has called me heavenward in Christ Jesus" (Phil 3:13-14). Here is the writer of almost half of the New Testament saying that he had not arrived at Christian perfection, but was ignoring the past and pressing on toward the prize. What is that prize? It is heavenward movement in Christ Jesus.

If we dwell on our past sins, it puts us in the frame of mind that we had when we committed them. That does not move us into the future. Instead, we need to forget the past failures and focus on Jesus and how He can transform us inwardly. The inner goal that will move us forward from our sinful past is to set our attitude to be as pure as Jesus will make us. Even if we don't feel like we are pure; even if we don't feel like we deserve God's purity; we need to ask for His holiness in our hearts and minds. Jesus makes us holy by giving us His Holy Spirit.

How do you feel about purity and being holy? Is there internal resistance to the thought of being completely pure and free from sin? Are there worldly things you are not ready to give up just now? That's too bad; because if we are willing to embrace purity, there is super-strength available from His goodness. We are given strength when we meditate on the concept of His purity and goodness. Think about how it would feel if every cell, every erg of energy in your body were pointed toward Christ and His goodness. We cannot defend evil. We cannot defend our protection of some bad habits or the bad habits of others. Rather, we are to place all of these on the altar of our hearts and let the pure fires of the Holy Spirit burn them up.

If I could write praise and worship about the purity of God, the words would go something like this: *Oh, to be filled with the purity and goodness of God! Is there any better feeling in this life? The freedom from all that wars against my soul brings with it such a release of joy that it cannot be contained. This purity gives me the strength of ten people. With it, I can live unshackled and free to praise my Heavenly Father without remorse over past sins. The future looks bright and it seems that nothing can stop me. My best days are ahead of me! Surely there will be tests to overcome, but Jesus is my Source and with Him I have the internal power to do it! I am sitting on a nuclear generator of purity. All that I want in this life, all that I really seek is realized, as I ponder this great gift. God loves me and I am significant to Him. I give thanks to Jesus for making it possible. What amazing grace! I will treasure this time.*

What about you? Is that your desire? The help from heaven we all need and want comes to us through the manifestation of the Holy Spirit, which is the purity, love, and goodness of God.

The Wrong Identity

As finite humans, we all misidentify God. No one knows Him completely because of His infinite nature. However, we were born with a knowledge of God and know enough about Him from the Bible to correct bad theology when we hear it. Many Christians have added or subtracted character traits of God to those which are clearly taught in Scripture. We do this to our detriment. If we misidentify God, we won't recognize His Holy Spirit or His gifts. What's worse, we end up not knowing who we are. Because we are made in the image of God, we become more like that which we worship. Consider the armies of ISIS believing that God would have them kill Christians in grisly ways. That barbarism is attributed to God and so members of ISIS become barbaric. That is an extreme example.

A more practical example involves the source of our own identity and self-worth. For years, part of my identity and self-worth involved the win-loss record of my favorite sports teams. If they won, I could feel good about myself. If they lost, I would feel bad and get the sense that something in my character was lacking. My self-worth was, and sometimes still is, tied up in what other people think about me. If we are trying to please other people, even if we don't agree with them, then they control our concept of identity and self-worth. Unless we get our self-worth, moral approval, and identity from the authentic Christ, we will never be sure of who we really are.

But what if we have a misunderstanding of who Christ is? What if we believe that God hates us because of our sin and that He would delight in sending us to hell? Some believe that God is always looking at them critically and in an accusing way. Many of these Christians cannot forgive themselves because the God of their minds has not forgiven them. They are stuck in self-loathing that God never initiated. Someone said that many Christians live as kidnapped and imprisoned royalty - not knowing they are free in Christ. Because they don't know God's true identity, they suffer through depression, never measuring up to what they believe is God's standard for them.

Jesus told a story about a man who thought his master was greedy and took things that did not belong to him. So he hid the money entrusted to him and gave it back when his master returned. This man stood condemned because he projected his own character flaws on his master. In the parable, the master was God and greedy servant was a person who misidentified God. We cannot think cruel thoughts about God and be happy because we become what we worship. If we believe God is stingy and judgmental, that is what we will become.

No matter how long we have been deceived, we can interrupt a bad life by finding God's true identity. Don't let the devil trick you into believing lies about God. The Bible gives us ammunition to confront our bad feelings about God with the truth. Read the book of 1 John with the idea of discovering God's true identity. Notice that the last verse of the book says, "Dear children, keep yourselves from idols" (1 Jn 5:21). That admonition is really saying, "don't misidentify God." There is so much more to this, but I think you get the point.

Let us pray: *Heavenly Father, please open my mind and heart to the truth about Your identity. Forgive me for any bad thoughts I have had about You. Help me to see clearly who I am in Jesus Christ and help me to enjoy life as You have intended. I thank You for Your great love for me. Amen.*

Does God Working in Me Affect My Free Will?

"For it is God who works in you to will and to act according to his good purpose" (Phil 2:13). This verse of Scripture, quoted earlier in the book, goes much farther in crediting God with our internal motivation than we are likely to do. Here are some questions that came to my mind when I thought about this statement:

- Does God work in me to will and act, even if I don't feel it or sense it?
- Must I apply my faith to increase this action or receive a benefit to my conscious mind?
- How can I know what God's "good purposes" are?

In short, the answers are: "Yes," "Yes," and "by studying His Word." But what about free will? The Biblical statement about God working in us to will and to act seems to negate human free will. How is human free will reconciled to God's sovereign will? In answer, people are free to do anything they want to do. Jonathan Edwards, the early American theologian, said that we do that which we are most inclined to do at a given moment. Edwards maintained we have never chosen to do anything in our lives against our own strongest inclination at that given moment.

As an example, I may not like going to work. Instead, I may want to stay home and watch videos, all things being equal. But all things are not equal. I have bills to pay and a family to support. When I weigh the possibility of bank foreclosure on my mortgage along with the daily needs of food and clothing for my family, I end up deciding that I would rather suffer the discipline and rigors of work than to go without food or shelter. Similarly, there are cases where we do things to please a loved one that we would not do on our own because their love or approval is more important to us than our own plans for that particular time. All of this is to say we do what we want to do 100 percent of the time.

So the question about God's sovereignty over our actions boils down to this: Who controls our wants and desires? Why do we want what we want? Can we truly have a thirst for God if He doesn't put that in our hearts? Can we make ourselves love God when we don't really love Him? The Bible makes it clear that until God regenerates our hearts, we cannot love Him or desire His righteousness. We may want civic righteousness to get public approval or to feel good about ourselves or to live without conflict. But we will not be motivated to want God and His holiness unless He is living in our hearts.

This is the key to understanding human free will: just because I don't know that God exercises control over everything (including my wants and desires), doesn't mean He isn't doing it. If my limitations prevent me from knowing everything and controlling the future, why should that limit God from doing it? I would never know He wields such power. But ignorance on my part has no effect on God. He can still do all He wants to do. Most people who stanchly insist on the freedom of their will do so with incomplete knowledge of God's capabilities. They may believe God is limited in some ways. But nothing could be further from the truth. Of course, there is much more to this debate and I don't want to get us off track.[2]

Let us pray: *Lord Jesus, I ask for faith to believe in Your work inside of me, even when I don't feel it. May I grow in Your grace to the point where I stop questioning Your sovereignty and instead, thirst for Your righteousness.*

---

[2] If you want to get into this subject deeply, I would highly recommend the book, *Freedom of the Will*, by Jonathan Edwards.

Please put the right wants and desires in my heart. I trust You to do it. Amen.

The Impossibility of Self-Help

When people look inward, they often want to fix what they see is wrong. Self-help books sell very well because of it. If I can fix myself, there is no need to have anyone else looking at me in a judgmental manner when I come to terms with my faults. Unfortunately, many of us have found there are limits to the lasting success of self-help. One achievement seems to turn up three new deficiencies.

Andrew Murray said, "Self serving God is more dangerous than self refusing obedience to God." What did he mean? He meant self would always serve itself. Self cannot serve God. Even when self gets the notion it wants to do good, it is only the self's idea of good. It is not God's idea of good. That is because the self is in competition with God. If self can heal and fulfill self, then we are to worship self. So God is obligated to defeat this idol and bring its self-effort to frustration.

Murray wrote, "I have never mentioned exertion or struggle, because I am so entirely convinced that our efforts are futile unless we first learn how to abide in Christ by simple faith." Discouragement and disappointment are the condition of many Christians because: "They have tried in the power of the flesh to conquer the flesh – a wholly impossible thing. They have endeavored by Beelzebub to cast out Beelzebub – this can never happen. It is Jesus alone who can subdue the flesh and devil."[3]

If we want receive help from heaven, we can only have it through the power of abiding in Jesus Christ. A wise minister recommended we need to use the same method that first brought our conversion to Christ – laying aside all of our efforts to justify and cleanse ourselves – and simply trust the Lord Jesus to grant to us His life and peace. Yet after this and perhaps years later, we still want to do everything ourselves. But even then, if we will go to the inner chamber of the heart, however cold and dark our hearts may have become, and wait expectantly for

---

[3] Andrew Murray, *Andrew Murray on Prayer* (New Kensington, PA: Whitaker House, 1998) pp. 161-162.

Jesus, He will come. We cannot force ourselves into the right attitude. Instead, we are to bow low before Jesus and confess that He is our only hope. We have to trust Him in a childlike way to have mercy upon us. We have nothing; He has everything.[4]

Listen to what the Apostle Paul says about this: "I would like to learn just one thing from you: Did you receive the Spirit by observing the law, or by believing what you heard? Are you so foolish? After beginning with the Spirit, are you now trying to attain your goal by human effort?" (Gal 3:2-3). The lie that we Christians believe is that at conversion, God has granted us grace and forgiveness and set the score back to zero, relative to our past sins. We believe it is now up to us to take this wonderful gift of salvation and make good of it. Then, at the end of our lives, we will give this great gift back to God with interest.

But that is not how God planned it! It is not one-and-done. He who saved us is able to constantly keep us saved. He who cleansed us is able to continue the cleansing process through every one of our future sins! Jesus wants to partner with us in everyday life. We need to let God do what only He can do. And yes, we have responsibilities too. But our human self-effort can never change us. Only by simple faith and abiding in Christ can we appropriate help from heaven and the divine victory God has for us.

Let us pray: *Lord Jesus, help me to lay aside my incessant desire to control everything. May I relax in Your strength and believe that You can change my heart for the better. I ask this in Your name, Amen.*

The Role of Struggle and Effort

It may seem that I am advocating a passive approach to spiritual life and faith, where "believing" is devoid of struggle or effort. That is not the case! You may have heard "Let go and let God." That is the opposite of "God helps those who help themselves." Each statement, if carried to its logical extreme, is out of balance. Rather, we must live in a spiritual tension. This tension comes after God regenerates our hearts (after we are born again in the Spirit) and then involves both believing God and doing what He tells us to do. Jesus said if we love Him, we have

---

[4] Ibid., p. 163.

an obligation to obey Him. That obedience requires discipline. It is a combination of active and passive faith.

Sometimes we need more of God and sometimes we need less of ourselves. The apostle Paul talked about "Christ in you, the hope of glory" (Col 1:27). Born again Christians already have the perfect Christ living inside them. There are times when we simply need to get quiet and align ourselves with Jesus who has already overcome our problem. He may jettison things in our hearts and minds that are making our problem worse. We must cooperate with Him by keeping our focus on Jesus.

There are a number of books on spiritual disciplines. If we are to understand this correctly, there is nothing we can do on our own that will change anything inside our hearts. That is God's job. Our job is to show up in His presence with believing expectations. Spiritual disciplines help us to do that. We are to place ourselves in a position to receive what God has. If we fast, it is to go into His presence. If we pray, we are putting ourselves in His presence. If we study the Bible, we are putting ourselves in His presence. And so on with the other spiritual disciplines. Waiting in His presence with expectation is the position needed to receive what God has for us.

Consider the risen Christ is like a nuclear breeder reactor, emitting the radiance of love, light, joy, peace, patience, and all the other fruits of the Holy Spirit. This analogy is important, so I will explain. A breeder reactor creates more nuclear material than it consumes.[5] Our analogy is that as we Christians sit in the presence of Jesus, we are irradiated with the Holy Spirit and His transforming radiance. Exposure to the radiance of His grace changes us from the inside out. People noticed that the unlearned disciples had been with Jesus. We too will become more like Him, the more we wait in His presence.

We get in trouble when we consider ourselves to be mercenaries of God, doing His work for Him, without Him. Our initiative must first be His initiative. We need to be like the Israelites in the desert when they were following the cloud of God, "In all the travels of the Israelites, whenever

---

[5] Scientifically, this occurs as Uranium 238 is irradiated by Uranium 235 and generates a new element, Plutonium 239.

the cloud lifted from above the tabernacle, they would set out; but if the cloud did not lift, they did not set out - until the day it lifted" (Ex 40:36-37). God wants to be the Leader in every decision, every conversation, and every prayer. We must sense His presence similar to the cloud for the ancient Israelites. There must be a spiritual tension as we pray always in every circumstance, speaking with Him about our work and play.

When the people asked Jesus about the work they needed to do for God, Jesus answered, "The work of God is this: to believe in the one he has sent" (Jn 6:29). The job of believers is to believe. We need to have faith that God is able to make the changes in us. Our "work" is to wait on Jesus in His presence daily.

* * * * * *

Looking inward, we must prove to ourselves that waiting in God's presence, relying on Him alone, is necessary to receive help from heaven. God is not our personal assistant to us. He is the Prime Mover, the First Cause, and the Originator of all enduring good actions we can make. He is first and we are second. When we quit trying to live a godly life according to our rules, and instead, abide in Christ in faith and trust, we will live a godly life that pleases Him.

Let us pray: *Dear Lord Jesus, thank You for saving me in spite of my own efforts. I ask You to help me abide in Your presence in my quiet times each day. I look forward to absorbing Your transcendent qualities and radiant love as I wait on You. May I be filled with expectation and faith that You will touch me in some personal and intimate way. May Your touch motivate me to do Your will and influence my circle of friends and family for Your kingdom. For this I thank You and praise You. Amen.*

Part 3 - Seeking Help from Heaven

Prayer brings help from heaven. The Bible tells us to pray continually (1 Th 5:17), yet we don't pray. And many of us have the wrong attitude about prayer, viewing it as a duty or a burden. If we understood prayer as our highest joy, our greatest privilege, and our reward from heaven, we would pray longer and more often. Prayer is a conversation where we both talk and listen. For a long time, I didn't pray unless I was in trouble. Then, I would repeat a one-word prayer - "Help!" You may have used that one as well. Now, I find myself praying quite a bit. I have learned four basic steps of prayer.

Step 1: Talk to God

Sometimes the obvious escapes us. If we want help from heaven, why not talk to the Creator of heaven? It seems prayer is the last thing we try after everything else fails. God invites us to pray. Jesus commanded us to pray. So prayerlessness is a sin! As such, our lack of praying carries a great cost. There are vast numbers of people who are perishing eternally because of it. Our own progress is hindered because we refuse to pray.

We consult our smart-phones and computer search engines more and more each day to ask every question from where to eat, to what to get our spouses for their birthday. If we would simply turn these questions toward the Holy Spirit, we would be surprised at what type of answers we will get. In fact, many people experience "beginners luck," where God will go to extreme lengths to show them He is there and wants to interact with them in secular activities. God is not confined to Sunday morning church. Every day, minor miracles happen in answer to prayer: money will show up unexpectedly; a parking place will open up; sick people will get well; the home team will win (yes, people pray about that!). We feel a sense of wellbeing because God has touched us.

Jesus said, "But the Advocate, the Holy Spirit, whom the Father will send in my name, will teach you all things and will remind you of everything I have said to you" (Jn 14:26). At first, it may only be problems we share with Him. But over time, He wants to "teach you all things." Jesus uses the word, "all." That means *everything*. Think about it. Math, science, relationships, love, competition, spirituality, sin, and everything else in the human experience is part of our learning process with the Holy Spirit. Nothing is out-of-bounds. And He has perfect advice!

So why don't we talk with God? Obviously, we don't *want* to talk with God. Some people avoid God for the same reason they avoid the doctor - they are afraid there will be bad news. Some of you may be saying, "That's not true, I've tried to talk with Him and He doesn't listen to me." Really? Here is what Jesus said: "But I tell you that men will have to give account on the Day of Judgment for every careless word they have spoken. For by your words you will be acquitted, and by your words you will be condemned" (Mt 12:36-37). Jesus is saying that there is a divine recorder that captures every careless word that we speak and that these will be played back on the Day of Judgment.

Instead of looking at this negatively, consider the flip side. God hears and records every word we utter. If we pray, God is hearing and recording that prayer. You and I can be assured that God hears everything we say. What a comfort! God hears me! He hears you! To speak with God, we simply need to open our mouths. We don't have to be in church. We don't have to be on our knees. We can talk and Jesus hears us. Let's use this power for good. Let's pray all of the time; talking with God about what is going on, how we feel, or what our decisions should be. There should be no limit to our conversation.

For example, a conversational prayer of mine may sound something like this: *Heavenly Father, thank You for the incredible opportunity of life You have provided. Lord, You said our work is to believe in You and that*

You would do what is impossible for us to do. I'm praying right now You teach me how to abide in You in simple faith and trust. Show me how to enter Your presence and wait as You fill me with Yourself. Teach me how to think and pray Your way. Teach me to hand over all of my problems to You and to walk through them with You leading the way. Keep me protected from evil as I learn Your ways. I trust You to fight the enemy for me. May I never return to the one-dimensional self that I have been before knowing You. Thank You, Jesus, for loving me enough to never leave me. It is in Your name that I pray. Amen.

This is not a set prayer. In fact, I made it up as I went along. My point is that there is a deep, rich, exciting life of prayer waiting for us if we take everything to the Lord and share it with Him. If we desire help from heaven, the best way to get it is to ask for it!

Step 2: Listen for God's Answer

When you set time apart to pray, expect to meet with God, personally. Expect He will solve all of the logistical problems associated with this meeting. Expect a message from Him specifically for you. He is addressing your DNA. We forget that He can be specific and detailed with us. If you get in the habit of listening to God, you will be amazed at the wisdom He will give you.

Sometimes, we need to pray first and sometimes we need to listen first. If we are to have a conversation with someone, we cannot do all of the talking. By definition, a dialogue involves words (*logos*) between or across two (*dia* from the root *duo*) people. At some point in our conversation with God, we will need to listen. The Psalms are full of examples of listening to God. In many cases, this listening process involves waiting in God's presence. "I wait for the LORD, my soul waits, and in his word I put my hope" (Ps 130:5).

We are not accustomed to the waiting process. If we are alone in silence, we fill it with music, computer games, email, or mental activity. We seldom get quiet and wait for God to speak to us. For that reason, God must use our circumstances to get His point across. How much simpler it would be if we could just hear Him speak to us directly. And no, I am not talking about audible words. I am talking about an inner knowing

God gives people who listen to Him. Jesus said His sheep hear His voice and follow Him (Jn 10:27).

Listening to God saves time and useless effort. "Unless the LORD builds the house, its builders labor in vain" (Ps 127:1). In modern terms we could say, "Unless the Lord approves of our marriage plans, we are in for a rough time." Or, "Unless the Lord directs our job search, we won't find our life's vocation." And I can say, "Unless the Lord directs the writer, the words will fall flat." We are to wait on God and follow His lead rather than to strike out on our own. The Israelites made this mistake: "But they soon forgot what he had done and did not wait for his counsel" (Ps 106:13). Today, we are making the same mistake. We do not wait for God's counsel. That is why many people are frustrated, depressed, and have unfulfilled dreams.

Jesus spoke to His disciples, "Do not leave Jerusalem, but wait for the gift my Father promised, which you have heard me speak about" (Acts 2:4). That gift was power from God when the Holy Spirit came upon them. The disciples gathered in the upper room to seek God's personal presence. They were willing to wait for the Lord in prayer indefinitely until He showed up with the gift of the Holy Spirit and power. Afterwards and under the power of the Holy Spirit, 3,000 people were converted to Christianity in one day!

We need to learn when God speaks to us, it isn't just words. It is power in the Holy Spirit. Our listening isn't passive. We are waiting, expecting, believing, and tuning all of our spiritual listening capabilities toward heaven. Jesus said, "If anyone has ears to hear, let him hear" (Mk 4:23). Jesus was talking about spiritual ears listening to what God is saying. We all have ears and most people can hear. But very few are listening to what God has to say to us. Hearing from God, in the presence of God, allows us to receive an unbroken supply of help from heaven.

How Do You Listen to God?

I would like to find out how you listen to God. But since we can't have a conversation, it may be helpful just to explain how I do it. To prepare for my heart to receive what God has for me, I first have to clear out the obstacle of sin that separates me from Him. That takes me to the atonement of Jesus for my sins. I quietly confess any sins that come to mind and ask for the blood of Jesus to pay for every one of my sins. Believing the sin barrier has been bridged by Jesus, I can open myself to the presence of God. Once in God's presence, I wait and I listen. It may take time, but God will speak to my problem either through imparted thoughts in my head or simply a "knowing" that lines up with Scripture.

I'm not perfect at this, and sometimes, God has had to use dire circumstances to get my attention. I have to also confess that I have sometimes pretended not to hear God when I actually did. When God whispered, "Don't drink that caffeine," or "Don't eat that late night snack," I had to make a decision to either follow Him or pretend I didn't hear Him. Maybe God hasn't put things like that off limits to you. But what about, "Don't flirt with that person at the office," or "Don't read that racy book or magazine or Internet article," or "Don't gossip about that person, pray for them instead," or "Tell the clerk he gave you too much change." How do you respond? Many of us tend to ignore the words from God that we don't want to hear. However, if we really want help from heaven, we need to be prepared to listen intently to all God says and then obey Him.

Still Don't Hear from God?

If you have talked with God in prayer and have believed He is able to answer you, and you still don't hear from Him, what then? First, never stop believing you *will* hear from Him. Second, find a Bible and begin to read the Gospels – Matthew, Mark, Luke, and John. As you read them, imagine when Jesus says something, He is saying it directly to you. Listen to what Jesus says: "My sheep listen to my voice; I know them, and they follow me" (Jn 10:27). Substitute your name in that verse. "I listen to Jesus' voice. He knows me and I follow Him." When you read the letters of Paul, James, John, and Peter, substitute your name wherever they address the churches. These are personal messages from God to you!

During my devotional time, I have begun to read the Bible aloud so the words are no longer just in my head. They are being verbalized and spoken. Spoken words have power and speaking the Bible out loud helps us to hear the One who inspired those words. Letting God speak to us through reading the Bible gets the conversation going. It is like having prayer training wheels. We don't have to hurry through this process. We can take our time and let the words resonate in our minds and sink into our hearts.

Deep inside, we know the truth of God's Word and that helps trigger our ability to hear from God Himself. Little by little, we will begin to hear the Lord speaking into our lives, telling us, "This is the way, walk in it" (Is 30:21). I believe we can hear from Jesus, get answers to prayers, and receive the help from heaven we seek. We know God hears every word we pray. It is time we hear every word that He speaks back to us.

Let us pray: *Lord Jesus, I repent for not praying about everything and listening to You for answers. Please forgive me and help me to hand my life over to You for leadership. I pray now for the power to listen to Your guidance and follow it. May my conversation with You never end and may I delight in our time together. I pray also for those who do not know You or do not speak with You on a regular basis. May You inspire them to pray and listen to You, as well. Please bless them and open their minds to the truth, for I ask this in Your holy name. Amen.*

Step 3: Commit to Doing What God Tells You to Do

The Bible tells us to be doers of the Word and not hearers only (Jas 1:22). We do not need to be perfect in doing everything we hear from God, but we do need to be *willing* to do everything. Sometimes our independent human nature gets in the way. Sometimes we are lazy. Sometimes we pretend we don't hear Him. Those excuses are still the essence of sin – disobedience to God. But if we are willing to do His will, we can trust He will eventually give us the ability to keep His commands.

"He will keep you strong to the end, so that you will be blameless on the day of our Lord Jesus Christ. God, who has called you into fellowship with his Son Jesus Christ our Lord, is faithful" (1 Cor 1:8). Further: "For it is God who works in you to will and to act according to his good purpose" (Phil 2:13). I go back to these Bible verses again and again, and you should too. God Himself will work inside of us to do what He has commanded us to do. Saint Augustine prayed, "Grant what Thou commandest, and command what Thou dost desire" (*Confessions* 10, 29). He understood that God must grant us the power to do what He commands. That should be our prayer as well.

We need to get to the place where we argue with God less and less when He tells us to do something. When we delay and wrestle with Him, that window of opportunity fades. I have found this out the hard way countless times. The person who was ready to hear my apology regains their hardness of heart. The opportunity to give money or time has less impact on the needs of recipients, and so on. In short, the power that was there from God to move boldly gets weaker the longer we delay doing what He has told us to do. Receiving help and anointing from heaven involves quickly following His instructions!

Let us pray: *Lord Jesus, I thank You for Your patience with me. I know I haven't obeyed You in a timely manner. I have waited or argued or found some other distraction that has kept me from doing what You have commanded. Please let my heart be open and pliable in Your hands. May You grant me the willingness to act when You say to act. Thank You for motivating me and disciplining me. I say this to Your glory and in Your name, Amen.*

Step 4: Dream Big

When you think about the fact that you have a finite time on this earth, what comes to mind? Do you look back and think about all of the things you've missed – or do you focus ahead on the goals you still plan to achieve? Are you nostalgic or visionary? Have you given up on your original dreams? If God has given you a passion for something, have you decided it is just not practical? Or that perhaps you will get around to it "someday" but not now? I've heard it said that "someday" is just another word for "never."

When my dreams die and I'm afraid the window of opportunity from God has passed, I think about this Bible verse: "Now to Him Who, by (in consequence of) the action of His power that is at work within us, is able to carry out His purpose and do superabundantly, far over and above all that we dare ask or think, infinitely beyond our highest prayers, desires, thoughts, hopes, or dreams" (Eph 3:20 AMP).

Consider the phrase: "Infinitely beyond our highest prayers, desires, thoughts, hopes or dreams." I have bold prayers, thoughts, and dreams. But God is ready to carry out and do superabundantly far over and above anything that we would dare ask. What are we afraid to ask?

God is already willing to do it. What does that say about our asking? You know the answer: we do not have, because we do not ask God (Jas 4:2). That begins to get at the problem.

The words from Ephesians show that even when we do ask, it is far too small in scope. God has help from heaven in store for us infinitely beyond our highest thoughts. Our thoughts are way too small. That is why I say dream big! Ask for more from God than you would ever think possible. Someone said it is better to ask for a lot and get 50 percent of it than to ask for nothing and get 100 percent of it! But let us be wise in our asking.

In the old Disney movie, "Darby O'Gill and the Little People," Darby gets three wishes from the king of the leprechauns. Some people urge him to ask for a pot of gold. Darby wisely replies that he would also need the ability to enjoy it. Others say he should ask for a mansion. Darby replies that he would also need the help to clean it and keep it up. There is a cat-and-mouse sequence as the king of the leprechauns tries to get Darby to waste his wishes. The point can be made that except where there is a dire immediate need, if we pray or wish for material possessions instead of spiritual growth and understanding, we gain little or nothing of lasting value. Solomon asked God for wisdom and God granted his request. God also threw in wealth and honor, which were not requested but were included as a side benefit.

If you really want to receive help from heaven, why not ask for an expanding intimate relationship with Jesus that you could share with many others? When we seek to know Jesus rather than just get things from Him, we end up getting the higher gift. Jesus Himself assured us if we seek first His kingdom and righteousness everything else we need would be given to us. See if the results are beyond anything you were expecting.

Let us pray: *Dear Lord Jesus, I want to know You better. I commit to talk with You daily and listen when You respond. I further commit to do what You tell me to do, with Your help. I want to dream big and ask for more from heaven than I think I can handle. May I rely on You when I think I am in over my head. Please let Your Holy Spirit fill me so I may share Your gifts with many others. I pray Your kingdom spread like wildfire in these last days. I love You, Lord Jesus, and I ask this to Your glory. Amen.*

Part 4 - Eliminating Specific Obstacles

Receiving help from heaven is difficult if our path is blocked by obstacles we ourselves have created. In this part of the book, I want to share effective ways of overcoming specific obstacles through Jesus. It may sound like I've oversimplified the answer by saying that Jesus is or will be the solution to every problem you face. But that is the honest truth! Of course, stating the answer is easy. As you may have found, implementing the solution is more difficult.

Identifying Obstacles

Being blind to our problems is a blessing and a curse. God does not reveal all that's wrong with us at one time because it would overwhelm us. So we are blissfully ignorant of many of our faults. But when it is time to move forward and overcome problems that have kept us in darkness, we learn that there are more problems that we didn't know about. God reveals them little by little so that we can handle the load. Most of these problems were caused when we were trying shortcuts to achieve our version of the "good life." Using counterfeit methods to get only what Jesus can provide creates problems. Consider the following list of obstacles:

- Drugs and Alcohol
- Pride
- Condemnation
- Shame
- Worry

- Fear
- Prayerlessness
- Bad Motives for Prayer
- Harboring Secret Sin
- Defending Ourselves

- Lack of Holiness
- Denial of Truth
- Selfishness
- Desire to Fix Yourself and Then Go to God
- Ingratitude
- Negativism
- Living in Strife
- Lack of Love
- Having No Spiritual Goals
- Nostalgia
- Things (material possessions)
- Impatience

Just reading the list can make us tired – particularly if we know we must address these issues directly. But now is not the time to give up or quit reading. There is real help from heaven if we will simply persevere. Rewards from heaven are just the opposite of this list. In heaven, there is no shame, condemnation, impatience, lack of love, bad motives, denial of reality, and so on.

Look at it this way: you will do something with the rest of your life, good or bad. Why not invest your time in tackling tough problems and making things better, no matter how long it takes? What more important thing do you have to do? It reminds me of what Peter said to Jesus when Jesus asked the disciples if they were going to leave Him: "Lord, to whom shall we go? You have the words of eternal life" (Jn 6:68). We need to realize that there is no alternate universe in which we can live. God put us in this one and we need to learn to deal with it. Someone said the easiest way around trouble is to go straight through it. And that's what we will do here.

Removing Obstacles with Jesus

Jesus is called the Advocate. "And if any man sin, we have an advocate with the Father, Jesus Christ the righteous" (1 Jn 2:1). What is an advocate? He is an attorney on your side, a supporter or backer willing to plead your case before a judge. When Satan brings an accusation against us, Jesus is our defender. The Bible says Jesus lives to make intercession for us (Heb 7:25). No matter what problem we have, we can ask Jesus to pray for our deliverance. Jesus doesn't have to take time out of His busy day to do this. He lives to make intercession for us!

For the sake of this discussion, let us assume that there are answers to your problems and to my problems. Would you agree to that? If you do not agree, then reading this book is a waste of time, because its major premise is that there is help from heaven for every problem. It has been said that simply recognizing the problem is a large percentage of solving it. I would add that believing solutions to our problems exist is also an essential part of solving them.

Drugs and Alcohol

If you are using drugs and alcohol, you will have trouble hearing from God. As I write this, the sale of recreational marijuana is being legalized in several states. That is bad for those who think legalization means that it is safe. The active ingredient in pot has a much longer half-life in the brain than does alcohol, sometimes taking months to clear or metabolize. Science is showing that marijuana use is related to an increase in brain disorders. These will dramatically increase in the years to come.

To hear from heaven, you must be equipped to listen. Clouded by drugs or alcohol, our minds cannot discern the move of the Holy Spirit within us. Addictions of any kind enslave our hearts and minds, often requiring us to defend what we know is wrong. I realize God answers people who call to Him in the midst of their drug or alcohol abuse, often breaking the addiction. But that should not be the norm.

If you are serious about hearing from God and receiving help from heaven, recreational drug use and drunkenness must stop. If you don't believe that you can stop, let this be your prayer: *Lord Jesus, I pray for Your help in breaking my addiction and I ask You to lead me to healing. If that is through a program or support group, please give me the courage to go and humbly ask for help. If Your Holy Spirit will supernaturally deliver me from this desire, I beg You to do it! Lord Jesus, I am serious about being healed. Please fill the hole in my heart that longs for You. I pray this in Your name. Amen!*

I don't know about you, but I am sensitive to caffeine. It is easy to get addicted to coffee in an office setting because everyone drinks it. When the Lord indicated that I needed to give up caffeine, I resisted. But at one point, I couldn't tell whether it was the Holy Spirit stirring my soul or the caffeine! So, I have given up coffee, even though it smells really, really good sometimes. But if we are serious about hearing from

God, we need to be willing to put away anything that hinders our walk with Him!

Overcoming Pride

Our pride keeps us from approaching heaven to ask for help. Unfortunately, pride can take many forms and it hides from us better than any other sin. We all have pride, but most of us underestimate its extent. We can easily mistake our pride for duty, honor, achievement, and good works. And for some reason, we can see the ugly side of pride in others much more easily than in ourselves. Sometimes, the pride we hide is assigned to the motives of others because inwardly, those are our motives.

The sin of pride is what ruined Satan. Pride is the overlooking our complete dependence on a forgiving God who supplies everything. God not only gives us a place to live and work, but He can recall our life at any moment. But you've seen it happen when a gift is given to people. First, there is gratitude and thankfulness. After a while, there is expectancy. Then the gift is no longer considered a gift - it is demanded as a right! At some point, if the gift is taken away, there is rioting in the streets and blood will be shed. Our pride is emboldened because we fail to recognize God's gracious hand in every aspect of our lives.

Perhaps you have met people who were too proud to accept "charity." However, that's not the real issue, is it? The real issue is that they are too proud to accept the pity of others, because it implies that those giving pity are better in some way. Our pride tells us we are better than other people and certainly not worse. Our pride is so afraid of being embarrassed, we would do almost anything rather than admit our faults before God and other people. We cannot repent if our pride doesn't let us acknowledge our sin. And that is where we have an impasse, because no unrepentant person will enter heaven.

The antidote to pride is humility. But we cannot be truly humble by our own willpower. Humility is the result of entering the presence of God and actually experiencing His holiness juxtaposed against our unholiness. Let that thought sink in for moment. Have you ever felt very, very small and profane? Until then, we can only *act* humble and do things that show humility. But we cannot *be* humble until we have

41

met the majesty and holiness of God. You and I need to pray for this gift! The Pharisee who thought himself better than the tax collector was not justified by his prayer to God. Rather, the repentant and humble tax collector went home justified with answered prayer (Lk 18:10-14). Herein lies the answer to help from heaven. God is willing to help you if you will simply acknowledge your sad state of blind pride before Him. All of us are guilty. But all of us can stand redeemed by the virtue of Jesus Christ. We must enter His presence, so let's do that right now.

Lord Jesus, You know the battle I face with my own pride. Help me to overcome this enemy of my soul. Show me Your righteousness and majesty in contrast with my own lack of purity. May this vision give me the experience of humility and break the grip of pride on my life. After this is done, I ask for Your reassurance of my worth in You. Amen.

Freedom from Condemnation

Whenever we break God's law, we incur real guilt - whether we feel it or not. Some people only trust their feelings and are deceived, either by false guilt or by not feeling any guilt. A sociopath, for example, doesn't feel any guilt for even the most heinous of crimes. However, most people are very sensitive to the feelings of guilt and condemnation. That is why political correctness and peer pressure are so powerful today. People will go out of their way to avoid any condemnation.

The devil uses condemnation to make us feel terrible about our sins and afraid to ask for help from heaven. His solution is for us to hide our sins and hope we are not exposed. But time will not heal our guilt.

On the other hand, God uses the Holy Spirit to *convict* us of our sin. This conviction differs from condemnation and is not meant to keep us in hiding with our faults. Rather, it is meant to lead and empower us to repent from whatever the sin is and seek the forgiving love of Christ. Conviction is a positive force meant to help us move into spiritual freedom. We are promised: "Therefore, there is now no condemnation for those who are in Christ Jesus" (Rom 8:1). If this is true, then our big question involves whether or not we are "in Christ Jesus."

How do we live in Christ? The simple answer is, through faith and trust. Jesus said, "I am the vine; you are the branches. If a man remains in me and I in him, he will bear much fruit; apart from me you can do nothing" (Jn 15:5). We abide in Christ by remaining in His love. He is the Vine that feeds us. Like branches, we draw our strength from His vitality.

The Bible says we are broken when we come into the world and we can't fix ourselves. So we shouldn't feel condemned that we can't. Our healing comes through Christ, who was broken for us so that we may live through Him. I realize this is a mystical truth, but it is a gift of heaven received by faith. Have faith and trust in Him the next time you feel inadequate or condemned. Your ticket to relief is to practice abiding in Christ.

Let us pray: *Lord Jesus, I submit to Your control over my life. Please show me how to abide in You. I desire to experience Your loving presence each day. I ask You to direct my attention toward You in an irresistible curiosity of love. Help me to repent for all of my sins. Remind me of Your forgiving sacrifice when condemning thoughts attack me. May I abide securely in You now and forever. Amen.*

Freedom from Shame

When we feel condemned without relief, it can lead to shame. Shame is a painful feeling of humiliation we get when we behave foolishly. Shame also produces a strong sense of guilt, embarrassment, unworthiness, or disgrace. Condemnation may come from the outside, but shame has its roots inside our identity. We are born with a soul and a sense of moral values. Deep down, we know right from wrong. And because of it, we can be shamed.

Once we have broken a moral law, our shame may keep us from taking a moral stand in the future. After all, we are guilty, and exposure would make us look like hypocrites. Satan is called "the accuser" and he uses shame to prevent people from standing for God. Have you ever heard something like this in your head: "You, of all people - how could you be a leader or tell anyone else what to do after the shameful things you have done?" And didn't Jesus say, "If any one of you is without sin, let him be the first to throw a stone at her" (Jn 8:7). Satan whispers these messages to keep us in shame.

Short-term shame may be healthy in preventing us from further immorality. However, long-term shame has a toxic effect on our personalities. Once feelings of unworthiness take root, it becomes very hard to believe and apply the good things God says are possible for us.

Before I was saved, I was afraid to go to God because of the many sins I had committed and the shame I had developed. The worst-case scenario kept playing in my mind: How would I admit my sins and explain my change of lifestyle to my friends and co-workers? I wasn't particularly worried about my family, since they wanted to see a change in me for the better anyway. But to confess I was wrong, morally corrupt, and in need of a Savior – that was so daunting. Had I not been desperate to find true life, I would have stayed away.

If we care more about what people think about us than what God thinks about us, we will stay in our shame. Our only path to freedom is transparent confession of our sin to God and humility before Him. "If we confess our sins, he is faithful and just and will forgive us our sins and purify us from all unrighteousness" (1 Jn 1:9). Don't let shame and fear of what people think keep you from being healed by God. Other people have just as many or more things to be ashamed about than you do. Instead of focusing on the shame of ridicule and embarrassment from people, we need to turn our attention to the fresh air of freedom and the great feeling of release and empowerment we will receive from Christ as He declares us "acquitted" from any guilt.

Let's believe what God says about us, not what people say about us! When we surrender our sin and shame to Christ, we give our reputations to Him as well. "Therefore, if anyone is in Christ, he is a new creation; the old has gone, the new has come!" (2 Cor 5:17). Direct help from heaven is available to you as soon as you ask for the courage to confess the sin that is keeping shame alive in you.

Let us pray: *Lord Jesus, I confess my sin of _____ (fill in the blank) that is keeping me in shame. I am embarrassed about this and have had trouble coming to You to speak about it. Help me to believe Your Word about the removal of this sin and my restoration to good standing with You. I pray to experience Your love as fully as possible. Please heal my soul and restore my identity in You. May my secret pride which has kept me in shame be eliminated from my life. I thank You and pray this in Your holy name. Amen.*

Freedom from Worry

Worry plagues us, often sucking the joy and happiness from everyday life. I remember the very weekend we moved into our new house, I found out my Father had terminal cancer. The exhilarating joy of our move evaporated instantly in the new worry and sadness about my Dad. Worry, when projected forward turns into fear and dread. I dreaded what would happen in the coming weeks and months as my Father wasted away with that awful disease. Yet my worry and dread didn't end there. I grew accustom to worry, as if it were a necessary part of life. I would take it with me and substitute the worry *de jour*. The desire to plan things out, control the future, insulating myself from pain led to "worry normalcy." It was normal to worry. I wouldn't notice it except for the high stress levels it created.

Jesus doesn't want us to live this way and He told His disciples, "Therefore I tell you, do not worry about your life, what you will eat or drink; or about your body, what you will wear. Is not life more important than food, and the body more important than clothes? Look at the birds of the air; they do not sow or reap or store away in barns, and yet your heavenly Father feeds them. Are you not much more valuable than they? Who of you by worrying can add a single hour to his life? And why do you worry about clothes? See how the lilies of the field grow. They do not labor or spin. I tell you that not even Solomon in all his splendor was dressed like one of these. If that is how God clothes the grass of the field, which is here today and tomorrow is thrown into the fire, will he not much more clothe you, O you of little faith? So do not worry, saying, 'What shall we eat?' or 'What shall we drink?' or 'What shall we wear?' For the pagans run after all these things, and your heavenly Father knows that you need them" (Mt 6:25-32).

I love that Scripture because Jesus was dealing with a very practical group. They wanted to know how they were going to put the next meal on the table. They were continually worrying about the logistics of life: what to eat, what to drink, and what to wear. We could add some items to that list: where to live, what to drive, how to pay for college, how to increase our credit scores, and so forth. Not much has changed. Yet Jesus put it all in perspective. He shows that if God cares for beautiful plant life, which has a very short life span, how much more will He care about us and provide for our needs?

When Jesus challenges His disciples not to worry, He is really asking, "Do you believe in God as your only source? Is He the One who clothes you? Is He the One who feeds you? Is He the One who protects you?" Those questions are also for you and me. If you think your boss is your supplier, you are only partially right. If you think your spouse is supposed to satisfy your needs, you are only partially right. We need to credit God as the Supplier of everything! If we are going to enjoy real help from heaven, we need to believe in God's direct role. The more you believe God is your direct supplier and source, the more He will confirm this to you *directly*!

So what do we actually gain from worry? Nothing! I can sense there are those reading this who don't agree. Many people think something *is* gained by worry. That's why they do it. In fact, they believe it is their obligation to worry about their needs. They believe it is irresponsible not to worry. By worrying about the future, they have done their part. Under this way of thinking, it is God's part to provide and our part to worry. Thus by worrying, we have "paid" for whatever we get.

Have you ever spoken with someone who tells you of the great worry they have had for their children? How they waited up those nights when the child was out on a date? Or the worry they had when the child was sick or getting ready for an exam? If truth serum were available, they would likely confess their worry was a payment to God for protection of their children. But when we understand what Jesus is saying - really understand it - worry is boiled down to unbelief! We don't think of it that way, but that's what it is. Worry and dread of the future can be linked back to our mistrust of God and what we think He has in store for us.

Everyone has had bad things happen to them or to loved ones. We did not invite this trouble, but it came upon us. Rather than seize upon every opportunity to draw closer to God, we sometimes use these bad events to justify pulling away from God and worrying about the future. Negative thinking relies on the old adage that if I don't expect anything good to happen, I won't be disappointed when it doesn't. How sad! Let me say this: If you don't expect help from heaven, you are unlikely to get it or recognize it when it comes. Faith is the key to receiving anything from heaven. Yet many people, including Christians, are in the grip of worry right now primarily because of unbelief.

Does that describe your situation? If so, your assignment is to believe God is able to protect you from your past and in your present, and to provide tomorrow's needs. You need to look up Jeremiah 29:11 and Hebrews 13:5 in the Bible and read those verses over and over until you believe them. These are promises of help from heaven. We need to increase our faith in God's provision and love so that even when bad things happen, those circumstances can drive us closer to Him rather than away from Him.

Let us pray about our habit of worry: *Dear Jesus, You have commanded me not to worry, but I worry anyway. Please help me to trust in Your protection, supply, and blessing. I am reminded that all things come from You and that You have a good plan for my life. Lord Jesus, You are my only Source. I give You all of my cares and believe my future with You is bright, no matter my current circumstances. Please break my habit of worry and unbelief with Your amazing love. Amen.*

Freedom from Fear

The devil wants you to live in fear so you won't enjoy your life. Fear often paralyzes us from doing anything good or bad. We can worry about how we are going to pay bills or whether the economy is going to revive or whether our kids will arrive home safely, but fear is more serious. Fear is defined as a distressing emotion aroused by impending danger, evil, pain, etc., whether the threat is real or imagined.

The last part of the definition is important: *whether the threat is real or imagined.* Many people fear things that, in reality, are not a threat to them. They have been tricked into believing that danger, evil, or pain is just around the corner. They waste large portions of their lives, give up their happiness and joy, and suffer stress because they haven't learned how to get rid of false fear. Now I am not saying that all fear is false - just the majority of it.

Fear of Death

Have you ever been on an airplane in severe turbulence? Invariably you will find some people reacting in fear and some people fast asleep! I remember being on a plane that hit such heavy turbulence that when the pilot finally landed, he received a standing ovation from the passengers. Yet even during the turbulence, some people were cracking jokes while others looked panicked.

Do you remember the story of Jesus and His disciples when they were out on a boat? "Without warning, a furious storm came up on the lake, so that the waves swept over the boat. But Jesus was sleeping" (Mt 8:24). Jesus was sleeping through a storm so bad that waves were splashing into to boat. It's one thing for the King of the universe to be self-assured through such an ordeal, but if we read on, we find Jesus was perturbed at His disciples for not have more faith and staying out of fear: "The disciples went and woke him, saying, 'Lord, save us! We're going to drown!' He replied, 'You of little faith, why are you so afraid?' Then he got up and rebuked the winds and the waves, and it was completely calm" (Mt 8:25-26). Jesus answered His own question about their fear by addressing His disciples as "you of little faith." Their small faith left room for fear.

Do you see that both worry and fear are caused by a lack of faith? Before I came to faith in Jesus, I feared death greatly. Even after my conversion, I would have occasional bouts with fear. But I heard a preacher who encouraged us to "do it afraid." We are not promised we will never *feel* fear. But even if we feel it, we are not to run away (either literally or in our minds). We are to stay and begin to pray and trust God like never before. That is the development of personal faith.

Until we are tested, our faith remains only a possibility. The proving grounds of faith occur when we are afraid but trust in God and do what we know to be right anyway. The antidote for fear of death is faith!

Fear of Punishment

Fear of death is one universal experience that people go through. But the Bible talks about another source of even greater fear – the fear of punishment for sin. This is the fear of encountering the holiness of God and receiving the just punishment for our disobedience. Deep inside we know that there will come a day of judgment for our sins. Yet many people who suppress this knowledge suffer from what they suppose is "irrational" fear or panic attacks. Our eventual date with divine judgment causes tremendous fear. Unlike an accident that could claim our life without moral judgment, divine judgment is specifically directed at our moral failures.

According to the Bible, perfect love casts out the fear of punishment. "There is no fear in love. But perfect love drives out fear, because fear has to do with punishment. The one who fears is not made perfect in love" (1 Jn 4:18). Divine punishment is directed toward unforgiven sin. Jesus made the connection between forgiveness of sin and love: "Therefore, I tell you, her many sins have been forgiven - for she loved much. But he who has been forgiven little loves little" (Lk 7:47). We cannot have perfect love until we receive forgiveness of our sins. Because of what Jesus did, I am free to receive the perfect love of Christ and be free from fear! But again, it takes real faith to believe in the atonement of Christ and to receive it.

* * * * * * *

Faith comes through hearing the Word of God and believing it. The Word of God spells out the Gospel, which declares our forgiveness through the sacrificial atonement of Christ. By believing and receiving His forgiveness, we experience the perfect love from heaven, which casts out fear.

Let us pray: *Lord Jesus, I pray that You give me faith and perfect love to overcome my fear. May I enter Your presence and trust You whenever I am afraid. May my heart feel Your perfect love and forgiveness even now. Thank You now and forever, Amen.*

Prayerlessness

The sin of prayerlessness is a major reason why we do not receive help from heaven. To open the gates of heaven, we must approach them in prayer and ask the God of heaven to help us. Several obstacles listed above keep us from approaching God, including pride, condemnation, and shame. If that is the trouble, let us be quick to go to Jesus and resolve these issues so we can pray effectively.

However, our fear of going into God's presence is not the main reason we don't pray. In America, most of us Christians don't pray as often as we know we should because of our apathy. We are people that know better. We have been with God. We have tasted the heavenly gifts. We know Who would receive our prayers. And yet, we don't pray. We complain that we don't have time to pray. But we do have time to watch TV, go shopping, play on-line games, look at social media, and all the rest. Prayer is so low in our priority system that it doesn't make the cut most days.

Some of this originates with the wrong idea of our own power to prevail in this world. Jesus told us that what was impossible for us is possible with God (Lk 18:27). Shouldn't that motivate us to go to Him for all of those impossible situations with people, relatives, spouses, money, jobs, etc.? Will it take a national catastrophe or a personal illness to get us to pray? If so, watch out!

God wants to talk with us. He is waiting and has been for a long time. His heart yearns to have us run to Him with everything and treat Him like a loving Father who cares about His children. He loved us from the moment He created us. But we have often rejected His outreach. Our independence and self-reliance has been more important to us than His constant and abiding love. Why else would we ignore Him except for brief prayers before bed or in early morning?

Before we resolve to pray more, let's put the power of our lives in the hands of Jesus. If we truly let Him lead us, we have no option as to where we get our marching orders than to go to Him in prayer. If He really directs us, then we will be in constant touch with Him. Now, more than ever, we need to become a people who pray. Pray for yourself. Pray for your neighbor. Pray for this nation. The hour is late!

Let us pray: *Lord Jesus, I want to share everything in my life with You. I give my life to You right now to do with as You please. Help me to trust Your command and to obey it! I love You, Lord. Amen.*

Bad Motives for Prayer

Some of us stopped praying because we didn't get the answers we wanted. Thankfully, God doesn't grant all prayer requests. Sometimes the answer is No! James 4:3 says, "When you ask, you do not receive, because you ask with wrong motives, that you may spend what you get on your pleasures." If God is going to give us gifts, He must be able to trust us not to go out and spend them foolishly.

Until our hearts are regenerated, our motives for prayer are selfish and manipulative. I was convicted by the Holy Spirit of "praying" with bad motives for sports victories for my home team. My praying was actually a form of superstition and witchcraft because I was trying to manipulate the outcome directly without God. Now, there is nothing bad about praying for victory if we ask Christ. But bad motives for prayer include putting a hex on the kicker, or hoping the other team will fumble the ball, or that the defenders will fall down. Once, when my team was losing, I began to root for the other team to put the "curse" of my support on them. Some people wear their lucky hat, or scarf, or shirt, etc. They think back to what they were doing or wearing when their team last won and try to do the same thing. This is an attempt at supernatural manipulation of events. We are not going through Christ, but taking matters into our own hands – a type of witchcraft that God forbids.

After Christ makes His home in our hearts, we have the ability to pray and act with good motives. We can give without expecting return and pray for others with power simply because we already have our fulfillment. Our prayers resonate in heaven because we allow the Holy Spirit to pray through us. "In the same way, the Spirit helps us in our weakness. We do not know what we ought to pray for, but the Spirit himself intercedes for us with groans that words cannot express" (Rom 8:26). We don't always have to pray in words. If the Holy Spirit prays from within us without words, God is able to answer His own prayers. Why He uses us at all, I do not fully understand. But He does.

If your motives are centered on yourself in prayer, you must ask God to change them. You will receive powerful help from heaven if your goal is to glorify God. If that is not your goal, ask the Holy Spirit to give you a heart for God. Ask that He pray His prayers through you and even if you have great problems of your own, ask that you become a blessing to others.

You may be thinking, "I am too worldly for this type of prayer. I have enough trouble of my own and I don't have the inclination to pray passionately for other people. We all have our problems." God's response to this is simply - "Try it!" What have you to lose? If God can do this miraculous thing in your heart, would it not be worth it?

Try praying this right now: *Lord Jesus, I come to You with a selfish heart, full of needs and wants. Your Word says You can change me on the inside to want what You want, and to have the joy You died to give me. I pray right now for Your Holy Spirit to invade my self-centered heart and do as You will with it. You must do all, for right now, I don't have the desire to do any of it. I am afraid it will hurt and I am not good with self-sacrifice. Please place the right motives in my heart to follow You and give me the grace and power to do it. I thank You and pray this to Your glory! Amen.*

Harboring Secret Sin

These days, secret sin is almost always sexual in nature. Whether it is lust, pornography, graphic romance novels, or sexual sin itself, we limit our help from heaven when we try to hide this sin. Part of the problem is that we are hiding the sin from ourselves. We don't want to acknowledge that our pet "problem" is a sin so we can continue to do it. And, like all sin, it alienates us from God.

There is a story in the Old Testament about the defeat of the Israelites in battle because of secret sin. "Israel has sinned; they have violated my covenant, which I commanded them to keep. They have taken some of the devoted things; they have stolen, they have lied, they have put them with their own possessions. That is why the Israelites cannot stand against their enemies; they turn their backs and run because they have been made liable to destruction. I will not be with you anymore unless you destroy whatever among you is devoted to destruction" (Jo 7:11-12).

The Israelites took things out of Jericho that were supposed to be destroyed. They hid them with their things as though the Lord would not know it. Similarly, when we harbor secret sin, we are lying about and protecting that which is devoted to destruction – in this case, our destruction. Think of secret sin as radioactive waste. When we hide that in our hearts, we will die.

We need to be honest about the "benefits" secret sin gives to us. Usually, sin makes us feel good at the time, but later we have remorse for it. The sin I am committing has no benefit to the real me. That is, I have no permanent place to store the "benefits" of that sin. At the end of the day, I am being used and deceived by forces that want to steal and destroy my soul. Meanwhile, the real me must wait for communion with God until this secret sin is exposed and put away.

To rid ourselves of secret sin, we must ask Jesus to help us. Don't fall into the trap of trying to justify or defend your sin. Instead, confess it to Jesus and let His atonement cover your past completely. I have found that by asking Jesus to replace the desire for secret sin in my heart with Himself, the desire to sin diminishes. It has been superseded by something better. This "replacement therapy" requires we withdraw our approval or even passive permission for the sin to exist in our hearts. That is where thinking about the eternal benefits has helped me. The real me wants eternal life with God. Why mess that up or interfere with my relationship with God through a temporary gratification of sin? It's just not worth it.

Let's pray: *Dear Lord Jesus, I harbor secret sin in my heart that is blocking communion with You. I recognize from this day forward, the sin which I thought was benefitting me in some way, is actually hurting the real me. Help me to replace the sin of _____ (fill in the blank) with Yourself. I know You want what is best for me and I do too. So I ask Your help to take the attractive glitter off my secret sin. Please restore my full and joyous communion with You. I ask this in Your holy name. Amen.*

Defending Ourselves

No one wants to be hurt. But when we try to avoid pain, we sometimes alienate our friends and family and block our reception of God's help from heaven in the process. Many of our defense mechanisms are ingrained so deeply in our minds and in practice that we will have to deliberately give them up in order to change. As a young boy, I remember going to the doctor's office to get a shot. I tensed up my muscle and the nurse told me that it would hurt a lot more unless I relaxed. My defense method was only making the pain worse.

At some point, we will need to be still and trust God to defend us. This requires standing firm in our active faith. Listen to what Moses said to the Israelites when the Egyptian army was pursuing them to the Red Sea: "Moses answered the people, 'Do not be afraid. Stand firm and you will see the deliverance the LORD will bring you today. The Egyptians you see today you will never see again. The LORD will fight for you; you need only to be still'" (Ex 14:13-14).

It's hard to be still in the face of danger. But that is what God told the Israelites to do. We can imply that they were to do it with the expectation of deliverance. They believed the Word of the Lord through Moses and divine intervention set the Israelites free from their bondage. This is the miraculous help from heaven that saved the day! By standing firm in our faith and trusting God with our defense, He can set us free from imprisonment in our own armor.

Let us pray: *Lord Jesus, I confess that am afraid to be vulnerable with You and with people. I realize that my desire to protect the real me is killing my relationships. Help me to trust You completely when my safety or security is threatened. Please give me Your grace and power to believe in Your protection of all that I hold dear. I pray this in Your holy name, Amen.*

Does this mean we are to disable our burglar alarms and get rid of any firearms we own? No, it does not. However, it does mean that we are to place our trust in God as our only Source of real security. If we are actually threatened, He will instruct us in what to do at the proper time.

Holiness: The Missing Ingredient

"For it is written: 'Be holy, because I am holy.'" (1 Pt 1:16). Holiness is God's ultimate plan for you and me, and has been from before the creation of the world. Is that your ultimate plan for yourself? Is holiness behind every prayer and earthly goal? If we were honest, most of us would admit it is not. In fact, it may the last thing we desire.

I remember taking a class at Cincinnati Bible Seminary back in the 1990s. Somehow, I had developed a reputation with the professor of having a sense of humor. So one class period, he asked me to tell a joke to the class. The class was populated mostly by pastors who were advancing their education through either masters or doctoral degrees. The only joke I could think of at that moment was one I had just read in a Reader's Digest. The joke was slightly off-color and when I told it, there was dead silence in the room.

It was at that moment I realized I was not remotely holy. Instead, I was quite profane. I felt a great embarrassment sweep over me, blood rushing to my face. I wanted to get up and leave the room, but my shame kept me glued to the seat. I remember leaving the class that night, walking into the clear night air and weeping before the Lord for my ignorance of His holiness.

No amount of trying to be holy on my part could have motivated me to change until I experienced firsthand the embarrassment of my un-holiness in that classroom that evening. I would not have known what I was missing. But once I was exposed to holiness and saw my profane position in relation to God's holy standard, I was humiliated. I knew my desperate need of God and His purity. How I sought Him that evening and the next day! When I went back to class, I apologized to my professor and he acted as though he didn't know what I apologizing for. If his reaction was genuine, then the Lord Himself orchestrated that whole event, mostly in my own mind, to help me experience His holiness.

I bring that story up to illustrate the point that holiness is an ingredient we don't know is missing until we are exposed to God's purity in a setting that cannot be misconstrued. Holiness is so vital to what God is doing in our lives that we cannot ignore it. Holiness is not an extra quality God adds to our character. Holiness is the distinctive part of His being that He wants to transfer to you and me – the Holy Spirit. And it is essential to receiving real help from heaven.

When we are born again, God's Holy Spirit abides within us. In fact, the amount of the Holy Spirit we can have is limited only by the degree to which we are willing to become holy. But because holiness is entirely the work of God, we cannot concoct it ourselves. "I the LORD am holy - I who make you holy" (Lv 21:8). God alone makes us holy. And when He does, He requires our carnal minds be crucified with Christ.

This is an embarrassing but essential process. Because there is some pain involved, it is like a post-graduate level spiritual course. This is a "take up your cross" moment. But willingness and faith on our part permits God to deliver His part. Pray for God's holiness in your life! God will reward you with more of His Holy Spirit.

Let us pray: *Lord Jesus, I ask that You expose me to Your perfect holiness. Make me holy as You are holy. Cover me with Your divine mercy as I realize where I stand and the filthiness of my sin. May Your holiness spur me to seek Your cleansing and flee to the safety of Your atonement for my sin. Please fill me with more of Your Holy Spirit – the Comforter. I thank You for Your love and forgiveness. Amen.*

Denial of Truth

Because truth can be painful, many of us deny it *to ourselves*. So what is truth? That is the question Pontius Pilot put to Jesus. Theologians tell us that absolute truth is reality as God sees it. The "lie" is not only the opposite of truth, but it is deception which obscures reality. The degree to which people buy into the lie is the degree to which they lose touch with reality. Taken to the extreme, the lie is insanity. This applies to both the individual and to society. The Bible maintains that believing the lie (or not believing the truth) is a moral fault for which we can be held accountable.

In many cases, the lie seems less painful than the truth. Sigmund Freud postulated that we can subconsciously suppress extremely painful events from our conscious minds. A person may have witnessed a terrible automobile accident and then had amnesia about that event. Or a young child of divorced parents may block out any of the fighting that he or she witnessed prior to the divorce. In this process, our minds are remaking our world into something we can deal with and control. The fear of death or other painful events "force" us to subconsciously protect ourselves from the pain of these emotions.

There's only one problem; this new version of the original event has been materially changed from what really happened. Freud further argued that the truth of the event, though repressed, cannot be completely erased from our subconscious minds. Thus, the truth can sometimes bubble to the surface in what is called a *Freudian Slip* or a dream, without our being conscious of it.

Although Freud was not a Christian, his insight into the suppression of truth follows a Biblical passage in the Book of Romans: "For since the creation of the world God's invisible qualities - his eternal power and divine nature - have been clearly seen, being understood from what has been made, so that men are without excuse. . . They exchanged the truth of God for a lie, and worshiped and served created things rather than the Creator" (Rom 1: 20, 25). *Exchanging the truth for a lie* is the problem I am talking about.

The ultimate denial of truth is to deny God's Word and to believe the lie. Satan's temptation of Eve began with the denial of God's Word. "He said to the woman, "Did God really say, 'You must not eat from any tree in the garden'?" (Gn 3:1b). No, God didn't say that. So Eve was safe. But then, "The woman said to the serpent, 'We may eat fruit from the trees in the garden, God did say, 'You must not eat fruit from the tree that is in the middle of the garden, and you must not touch it, or you will die." You will not surely die,' the serpent said to the woman" (Gn 3:2-4). *There it is*, a boldfaced lie – a direct contradiction of what God said.

The most direct method of receiving help from heaven is to resolve to face truth, no matter how dark or incriminating, through the help of Jesus. Jesus said that He is the way, the truth, and the life. It is not a coward's way out to rely on Jesus to face reality. He is reality. His Word is truth. When we believe what the Bible says about us rather than what our feelings tell us, we are embracing a deeper reality. This truth sets us free (Jn 8:32). The Bible says that Jesus died for my sins, that He loves me, and that I am forgiven and empowered with His righteousness. When I feel guilty or inadequate, I have to remind myself to confess any new sins, repent, and believe the truth. Almost instantly, I breathe easier.

With heaven's help, we can face that estranged spouse, family member, or former friend if we know that the love in our hearts will not be extinguished by what they say or do. Those people or circumstances do not have the power to shut off the fountain of love flowing to and from Jesus, even in the midst of our suffering. I can hear some of you saying – but aren't you substituting a false reality of your own by retreating into an insulated world of love in "Jesus." The answer would be "yes" if it were a false world of love. But if you believe the Bible, and if you have conducted personal business with Jesus, then the truth Jesus conveys to us is bedrock reality. This is the potent help from heaven that sets us free and conquers our feelings of guilt or inadequacy.

Let us pray: *Lord Jesus, please help me to face the truth about myself or my past that I fear. I believe Your Word is truth. I trust You, Jesus, to forgive every single one of my sins completely to Your satisfaction by Your atonement for them. Please lift the veil from my mind that keeps me from seeing reality clearly. I can do all things I need to do when You are strengthening me. Amen.*

Selfishness

If we didn't know better, selfishness seems to be the best way to get our needs fulfilled. We all need food, shelter, and money, right? Why is it bad to set our minds on those things and then go get them? People who do this are called industrious, hardworking, self-reliant, and productive. Aren't those virtues? Of course, they can be, depending on our motives. What is bad is the notion we are alone in our quest and no one else matters. In fact, the end result of selfishness is exactly opposite of what we expect, because instead of preserving our life, selfishness consumes it. Instead of making us happy, selfishness makes us miserable.

God is working on us to play well with others and share our toys because that is what He does. Selfish people cannot do that with joy. They worry that their possessions will be stolen or ruined. When we get right down to it, selfishness is a distrust that God will protect our interests - we don't believe He will supply our needs. It is not enough to look at selfishness as a human trait that simply cannot be helped. God perceives it as a sin! That was the sin of the wicked and lazy servant who buried the gift that his master gave him (Mt 25:24). When we are selfish, we see everyone else, including God, as selfish and greedy.

What about you? What if money were no object? Would you look at life differently? Would you loosen your grasp of material things? If so, why can't we do this before finding another source of income, and simply trust God completely for our supply? When we are focused on the earthly prize, we forfeit the heavenly prize. Christians, we don't have to compete with other people. We simply have to ask the Lord for His supply and believe He will give it. Think of the violence and bloodshed that could be avoided if everyone recognized we have only one real Source of supply!

Here is the irony: we must do the opposite of selfishness to bring abundance into our lives from heaven. It is counterintuitive but Jesus told us that if we want to get, we must give. That means turning the other cheek when someone strikes us. It means loving our enemies and praying for them. It means giving more than people ask or expect of us - going the extra mile. Yes, there is great risk. But there is great reward! Isn't that the exhilarating life that you and I have been seeking?

Let's put the ball in the other court and instead of asking God to meet all of our needs, let's see how we can serve Him and serve others. Jesus said that God already knows our needs and the best way to get what we want is to place God's kingdom and His righteousness first in our lives. Then all of the other things we need will be provided (Mt 6:25-34).

Let us pray: *Lord Jesus, I confess that I am a selfish person. I know in my mind that this is harmful to my growth in Your kingdom. Help me to trust You with my future completely so that I can become more generous in my heart with everything I own. May You work through me to break the grip of selfish concern that pervades my thinking. May I commit everything to You so that I have nothing left to lose. I ask this in Your name and to Your glory. Amen.*

Desire to Fix Yourself and Then Go to God

The Bible says, "While we were still sinners, Christ died for us" (Rom 5:8b). Do you get the impact of that? Christ died for my sin and your sin *before* we were cleaned up. He did it when we were still sinners. Many people who want help from heaven believe they first have to fix themselves to be presentable to a holy God.

But how are we going to get right with God, without God? When we put it that way, it does seem that we are getting the cart before the horse, so to speak. How can a tainted person fix the contamination in themselves? It is impossible. On a non-spiritual level, we understand that we can't clean a grape juice spot out of shirt with more grape juice. We need a *cleansing agent.*

But aren't we supposed to help God fix ourselves? Aren't we supposed to read the Bible more, go to church more, pray more, try to think pure thoughts, etc., if we want to get closer to God? Not exactly. Those actions are the *result* of closeness with God. They aren't responsible for bringing us to Him. God's gift to the unclean is to make them aware of their filthiness. We are then hungry and longing to be washed and cleansed from sin.

No amount of training, discipline, or good behavior can make our carnal nature ever serve God. The carnal nature is *completely* hostile to God (Rom 8:6-8). In fact, our carnal natures will do anything to stay in command of our minds – even promising to serve Christ. This deception will always end in failure. Andrew Murray taught that as long as the carnal nature had any influence in serving God, it would remain strong to serve sin, and that the only way to keep it from doing evil was to prevent it from trying to do good. It is depressing to the person trying so hard to fix himself or herself because it seems an impossible task. Indeed, without direct help from heaven, it is.

So how are we supposed to live a Godly life without the "self" participating? This problem has been around for a long time. Listen to how the apostle Paul dealt with it: "I would like to learn just one thing from you: Did you receive the Spirit by observing the law, or by believing what you heard? Are you so foolish? After beginning with the Spirit, are you now trying to attain your goal by human effort? Have you suffered so much for nothing - if it really was for nothing? Does God give you his Spirit and work miracles among you because you observe the law, or because you believe what you heard?'" (Gal 3:2-5).

The apostle Paul learned that human effort was futile in achieving spiritual results. Only *believing* God and allowing Him to prepare our hearts will fix what's wrong inside of us. Through our faith and trust in the power of Jesus, He will "move" us to follow his decrees and laws. Rather than try to clean ourselves up, we need to pray and believe that God can and will do it. He has promised to do it: "I will sprinkle clean water on you, and you will be clean; I will cleanse you from all your impurities and from all your idols. I will give you a new heart and put a new spirit in you; I will remove from you your heart of stone and give you a heart of flesh. And I will put my Spirit in you and move you to follow my decrees and be careful to keep my laws. You will live in the land I gave your forefathers; you will be my people, and I will be your God. I will save you from all your uncleanness" (Ez 36:25-29).

All of our previous efforts to be a good person will fail to change our own hearts. We are not going to be able to help God except to surrender our human efforts and by faith, let Him work within us. Our faith in His ability to change us will ultimately meet with success and we will be surprised by the abundance of His grace as He opens the windows of heaven to us!

Let us pray: *Lord Jesus, I am often ashamed of my behavior. So I have tried to clean myself up before coming to You. Sometimes, I have stayed away for weeks. Although this has never worked, I continue to do it. Please forgive my pride and autonomy. I know now I cannot fix the sin within me. Help me to wait on You humbly in faith and trust for Your cleansing. May Your blood wash me. May Your peace enfold me. May Your love restore my soul. I thank You, Lord Jesus for Your grace in redeeming me! Amen.*

Freedom from Ingratitude

My Father worked at a department store and when he went to New York City on buying trips, he would come back with presents for each of us little kids. We would run to meet him at the door with delight, wondering what gift we would receive. One time, he didn't bring any gifts and three children left him at the door and went away crying. That was the end of the gifts. In a small way, my Dad must have known what God feels like when we do that to Him. We look for the gift rather than to be with the Giver.

Believe it or not, ingratitude is a major offense against God and an obstacle to receiving help from heaven. Romans Chapter 1 gives God's response to ingratitude: "For although they knew God, they neither glorified him as God nor gave thanks to him, but their thinking became futile and their foolish hearts were darkened. Although they claimed to be wise, they became fools" (Rom 1:21-22). Those who do not give

God His proper honor and thankfulness are given over to their own darkness.

When we don't love God with thanksgiving, we are placing His gifts and the benefits of His creation higher than God Himself. Let me ask you, how thankful are you that God has taken your sin through Christ's atonement? If the answer is "not so much," then you have undervalued the cost of sin and its impact on your soul. Billy Sunday said, "One reason sin flourishes is that we treat it like a cream puff instead of a rattlesnake." Our ingratitude toward God is often overlooked because its root cause is our attitude of indifference toward sin.

Those who understand the penalty for sin have unbounded gratitude toward God when He forgives them. Jesus illustrated this point in a parable. "'Simon, I have something to tell you.' 'Tell me, teacher,' he said. 'Two men owed money to a certain moneylender. One owed him five hundred denarii, and the other fifty. Neither of them had the money to pay him back, so he canceled the debts of both. Now which of them will love him more?' Simon replied, 'I suppose the one who had the bigger debt canceled.' 'You have judged correctly,' Jesus said" (Lk 7:40-43). Our love for God is generated in large part by the knowledge and experience of our forgiveness in Christ.

Let us pray: *Lord Jesus, I thank You for Your complete forgiveness of my sin. As I contemplate the full scope of this forgiveness, I cannot help but be grateful and love You back. Help me to never take Your grace and mercy for granted. I pray this with thankfulness in Your blessed name, Amen.*

Negative Attitudes

Negativism is a state of mind that expects bad things to happen and suspects the universe is ultimately God-less. Often, our faith materializes what we expect to occur in our lives. There is the story of the traveler who met an old wise man as he was journeying to a new city. He asked the old man about the new city and what the people were like. The old man asked what the people were like in the city the traveler just left. "They are a bad lot, stealing what was not theirs, hard hearted, and mean." The wise old man said, "I'm sorry to hear that, because the people in the city just ahead are the same."

Later that day, another traveler approached the old man and asked the same question. Again, the old man asked what type of people lived in the city from which the second traveler had just come. "They are kind hearted, loving, and gentle people, full of concern for their fellow man." The wise old man responded, "You are in luck. You will find the same type of people live in this city."

And so it is true. Many of our expectations are fulfilled – good or bad. If we start with a negative attitude, it can ruin the best of intentions and fracture relationships. Instead of thinking the best of someone, negativism assumes the worst and assigns motives to peoples' actions that were never there. Pessimistic people find it hard to truly love, because they cannot truly trust. Worst of all, negative attitudes poison and destroy the person using them. They think they are protecting themselves from being hurt by believing that if you don't expect much out of life, you won't be disappointed when nothing good happens.

Without knowing it, pessimistic people are in the habit of believing bad things about God. They malign His character by assuming He has a bad plan for them or that He is not interested in their day-to-day lives. They may have had bad experiences in the past and assumed God was mad at them. Instead of taking good lessons from their hardships, they often blame God and only see the shallow aspect of pain. However, the Bible says that all things (even bad experiences) do work together for good for those who love God and are called according to His purpose (Rom 8:28).

Is God positive all the time? The answer actually is yes. The Bible says, "For no matter how many promises God has made, they are 'Yes' in Christ" (2 Cor 1:20). Even more telling is the description of the Lord of lights as follows: "Every good and perfect gift is from above, coming down from the Father of the heavenly lights, who does not change like shifting shadows" (Jas 1:17). There is no shadow in God. There is no doubting in God. He positively sustains the physical universe all of the time.

If you could go through life with a positive or negative attitude, which would you choose? Does your choice line up with your current attitude? Did you know you actually have a choice in the matter? We can actually change our attitudes from negative to positive by force of will and faith in Christ's ability to change us on the inside. It won't happen overnight because of the years we have spent developing our thinking patterns and habits. But our minds can be re-trained with positive thoughts if we choose to dwell in them.

Don't listen to that voice in your head, which continues to tell you nothing good is going to happen or that you are not being "realistic" when you have a positive thought. Tell that lying voice to back off and substitute your own voice with positive, Biblical affirmations about your future. Look up the good promises of God in the Bible and then repeat them out loud. Something good is going to happen to you today! You will find God if you seek Him with your whole heart. What does that really mean? It means that hope is possible; that love will triumph in the end; and that help from heaven is on the way. It's not corny. It's the realization of all our inner dreams and aspirations.

Let us pray: *Lord Jesus, please forgive me for thinking bad thoughts about You. I have sometimes doubted Your good plan for me and wondered if You were involved in my daily life. I have had negative thoughts about myself and my future. I pray You would help me live with a positive attitude toward You, my life, and those around me. May I not be derailed by negative circumstances, but instead, may those challenges energize me to believe You even more whole-heartedly for my deliverance! Amen.*

Living in Strife

A Christian pastor once told me about a man whose prayer life had disappeared. This man was a practiced prayer warrior who seemingly had been decommissioned. I was interested to hear the pastor's line of questioning. He asked the man how his relationship with his wife was going. The man was taken aback by the question but responded honestly that there was a lot of strife in the home. The pastor quoted this Scripture, "Husbands, in the same way be considerate as you live with your wives, and treat them with respect as the weaker partner and as heirs with you of the gracious gift of life, so that nothing will hinder your prayers" (1 Pt 3:7). Fast forward. When the man eliminated the strife between himself and his wife, his effectual prayer life was restored.

Jesus said, "Therefore, if you are offering your gift at the altar and there remember that your brother has something against you, leave your gift there in front of the altar. First go and be reconciled to your brother; then come and offer your gift" (Mt 5:23-24). It is God who brings up the remembrance of the conflict. When we are living in strife, where anger, jealousy, rage, and all of the other unseemly emotions are exposed, our prayers are hindered and ineffective.

One of the titles of Jesus is the Prince of Peace, which is the polar opposite of strife. Would Jesus feel comfortable sitting in your living room while you and your spouse were arguing? Well, neither would the indwelling Christ in your spirit. We are so far from Him during those times. If we want the anointing of God, where our words have His power to penetrate the world's force field around us and reach heaven, we need to eliminate strife.

Strife is used by the enemy to steal our peace and take us out of the household of God. Remember that King David wanted to dwell in the house of the Lord forever? (Ps 23). Well, we can't do that if our house is the staging ground for an ugly war. Anyone who wants to clearly hear from heaven must first eliminate strife from his or her household. Similarly, anyone who wants a ministry must eliminate strife as well. We cannot do this without God's help because it requires turning the other cheek, biting your tongue when you want to let it loose on someone, and trusting that God will sort out any injustice in His good timing.

Let us pray: *Lord Jesus, there are many times when I have allowed strife to rule my life. I pray You would calm my heart and set my mind on Your peace. You gave Your disciples peace, not as the world defined it, but a divine peace that passed all understanding. Lord, I ask for that gift of peace. May I be one of Your peacemakers. Any situation that has driven me into strife or that will drive me into strife in the future, I give to You now. Help me to overcome my temper and lack of self-control. Draw me to You, Lord Jesus, for I ask this in Your name. Amen.*

Lack of Love

It is definitional that people without God are those without love. Why? Because the Bible says, "God is love. Whoever lives in love lives in God, and God in him" (1 Jn 4:16b). The key point is that if you are living in love, you are living in God, and God is living in you. Love, living on the inside of you, resonates with God because it is His nature.

But let's be clear about the type of love we are describing. This love is not a reciprocal process that must be earned. Jesus said, "If you love those who love you, what credit is that to you? Even 'sinners' love those who love them" (Lk 6:32). Nor is this love simply that of a person *in love*. Some people love to be in love because of the way it makes them feel. When called upon for self-sacrifice, loyalty in spite of pain, and faithfulness during hard times, this selfish love evaporates. That is not Biblical love.

The best definition of love in the Bible comes from the well-recognized passage in 1 Cor. 13:4-7: "Love is patient, love is kind. It does not envy, it does not boast, it is not proud. It is not rude, it is not self-seeking, it is not easily angered, it keeps no record of wrongs. Love does not delight in evil but rejoices with the truth. It always protects, always trusts, always hopes, always perseveres." Notice by inference cynicism, cowardice, distrust, negativism, and impatience are opposite characteristics of love.

How many people outside of your family do you know that exhibit true love today? The list may be rather short. The Bible predicts the love of the great body of believers will grow cold at the end times because of multiplied lawlessness (Mt 24:12). We live in an age when spectacular crimes are not shocking anymore. Locks and security systems are required for all of our possessions. Even our identity must be protected, as digital thieves seek to steal our Social Security and credit card numbers. We have come to expect that very few people can really be trusted. If love always trusts, then the moral decline in society has dramatically reduced the supply of love. In short, our love has grown cold and we cannot hear from heaven because we don't have the currency of heaven in our hearts.

You and I need to be counter-cultural in this. We need to love intentionally when most people would not. With Jesus in our hearts, we have the Source of love living inside of us. We don't have to generate this love on our own. We simply need to let it flow through us back to God and outwardly to other people.

But what if love is lacking? What if we try to love and can't seem to make it happen? What then? If you have done business with Jesus in the past, call out to God to fill your heart with Himself anew. Believe His love is there! Believe the Spirit of God is spreading the love of His being through you. Even if you have tried and tried and failed in the past to live up to the standard of love you know God expects, there is hope for success. This hope comes from the promise: "Being confident of this, that he who began a good work in you will carry it on to completion until the day of Christ Jesus" (Phil 1:6). God will not give up on you or me until He has achieved His purpose: He wants to fill us with His holy love.

In receiving the help you need from heaven, God has thought of every detail in bringing you to perfection, and this includes the ability to love deeply. You don't have to know how He is going to do it; you simply need to believe that He will. If those stumbling blocks within us seem impossible to move, we need to believe God is powerful enough to move them and that He *is* already moving them. He will supply everything necessary. Your only job is to believe it and to wait expectantly for God to fill you with Himself. If you persevere, God will fill you with His great love.

Let us pray: *Lord Jesus, I ask to experience the full measure of love You have for me. May the radiance of Your loving heart penetrate any shell of protection I have used against You or Your kingdom. Let the heat of Your love melt any coldness in my heart. Teach me in the ways of Your great love. Give me a heart to share this love with everyone I know. I ask this in Your blessed name, Amen.*

Having No Spiritual Goals

If you have no spiritual goals, you are likely to achieve them. What? Another way of saying this is that without spiritual goals, we lack the focus needed to persevere in our faith. We have better success achieving those things we try for versus trusting dumb luck to succeed. Like Alice in Wonderland, if we don't care where we want to end up, it doesn't matter which way we go.

It's reported that college graduates with written life goals consistently achieved more than those without goals.[6] The same could be said of those with spiritual goals. Jesus made it clear: "But seek first his kingdom and his righteousness, and all these things will be given to you as well" (Mt

---

[6] Source: Gail Matthews, Ph.D., "Summary of Recent Goals Research" (Dominican University). For further reading: http://sidsavara.com/personal-productivity/fact-or-fiction-the-truth-about-the-harvard-written-goal-study

6:33). We are to set our sights on God's kingdom and His righteousness and then God will take care of the other material things we need.

Our minds wander through the day and we can be preparing for bed and realize we haven't thought about God once the whole day. Why? Because our hearts (goals) were somewhere else. We need to think about what we are thinking about. Are we pursuing God? Have you spent time anticipating, hoping, desiring, and planning for your rendezvous with Jesus? Do you regularly enter the presence of God in prayer? Quality time with God involves more quantity than quality. Help from heaven comes as we set our priorities on God.

When we press in towards God during times of hardship, we seem to let up once we have a breakthrough. God is teaching us that we need to keep the attitude of mind to press in after we've had our initial breakthrough. People do marriage the same way. They pursue their beloved until they are married and then act completely different afterwards. We can't just be thrilled with the chase. We need to finish strong. And that's where spiritual goals and discipline come in.

Andrew Murray preached that without spiritual goals, we will see little progress in becoming more Christ-like, more forgiving, kinder, and more loving. We may think that going to church and reading the Bible, agreeing with its concepts, and believing it will somehow, of itself, translate into a change of character inside of us. By experience, we find this doesn't work. The change comes only when we seek it. Remember, the scribes studied the Scriptures but were not changed by them because they did not have the spiritual goals Jesus taught.

If you desire help from heaven, set your goals to actively know the living Christ. Prayerfully think about meeting Jesus face to face. Wait on Him daily and let that time of anticipation and prayer be your highest blessing.

Let us pray: *Lord Jesus, I admit that I have not been diligent in setting and keeping spiritual goals. Instead, I have focused my attention on worldly pursuits and getting ahead materially. I repent from having the wrong priorities and ask Your forgiveness. Please guide me into the desire of heavenly goals and align my heart with Yours. Show me how to wait in Your presence with great expectation, for I pray this in Your name, Amen.*

Nostalgia

"Jesus replied, 'No one who puts his hand to the plow and looks back is fit for service in the kingdom of God'" (Lk 9:62). Nostalgia is defined as a bittersweet longing for things, persons, or situations of the past. To be nostalgic, we must be looking backward. Longing for the way things were more than the way things are or the way things will be shows we do not have faith that our lives are getting better. Rather, we think that the best years are behind us. This is the lesson of Lot's wife in the Bible - by looking backward with longing, we become frozen in time.

Now, I am not saying it's bad to look back at our past with joy. But if we stay there in our minds, and if we believe we are on the downward side of life, we hurt our ability to receive help from heaven. Heaven is now and in the future. The energy that fuels our hope is in the future, not the past. It is our union with Jesus Christ. The apostle Paul had to forget what was behind and strain toward what was ahead (Phil 3:13b). And so do we.

When I got my first job, I lived in an apartment building and met the maintenance manager who had served in World War II. He would get drunk almost every day and reminisce about the War and his time in India. Clearly, it was the highlight of his life. When he spoke about his time overseas, his eyes would light up and he would begin to re-tell stories of his combat service. As a young man from the Midwest, he was transported halfway around the world to fight in a worldwide war. His life had meaning and purpose. And he risked it to save his country. But everything from that point was downhill. He was living an anti-climactic existence. And so he drank to pass the time. What a waste!

If we desire help from heaven, we cannot mix it with nostalgia. Even spiritual nostalgia – the longing for great spiritual experiences we've had in the past – can hamper our now-relationship with God. Our strength is in the *present,* in the *presence* of the living God. Looking backward, we cannot see the open gates of heaven and the pathway to immediate help. We need "future-algia" where we face the future with bittersweet longing for heaven and God's closer friendship.

When we look backward, let it be to recall what God has done for us in the past in order to bolster our faith in the present. The Psalms contain a number of cases where the psalmist recounts God's mighty works of the past in order to build his faith in the present. Mary, the mother of Jesus, reminded God of His faithfulness to Israel in her song or "Magnificat" (Lk 1:46-55). But there is a difference between the recall of history and nostalgia. Nostalgic people want to reverse the present and go back in time. Faith-filled people want to use history for confidence to take on the present and have victory as they move into the future. Don't be stuck in the past!

When Christ comes to live in our hearts, the "aliveness" we thought was in the past is in the present. That is a major breakthrough in our spiritual journey and we find the opposite of nostalgia is hope. Christ gives us hope for the future in our expectation of becoming *wholly holy*. Let's face the future with excitement and joy knowing Jesus will provide help from heaven right now and in the future.

Let us pray: *Lord Jesus, help me to see with clarity the road ahead of me. May I value my future with You so much more than my past without You. Please give me the hope of greater and greater communion with You for the rest of my life. For this I praise You and thank You. Amen.*

Freedom from Things

Someone said that we are to love people and use things. But many times, we use people to get the things we love. You and I already know that money (or things) can't buy happiness. But people joke that with it we could afford to choose our misery. Unlike our grandparents, we don't attempt to fix broken things; we buy new ones. Unless consumers spend lots of money at Christmas, the economy will tank. Unfortunately, we have forgotten the real American dream was not about materialism. It involved religious pilgrims who were looking for a place where they could worship Jesus Christ in freedom.

Jesus told a story: "The ground of a certain rich man produced a good crop. He thought to himself, 'What shall I do? I have no place to store my crops.' Then he said, 'This is what I'll do. I will tear down my barns and build bigger ones, and there I will store all my grain and my goods. And I'll say to myself, "You have plenty of good things laid up for many years. Take life easy; eat, drink and be merry." But God said to him, 'You fool! This very night your life will be demanded from you.

Then who will get what you have prepared for yourself?' This is how it will be with anyone who stores up things for himself but is not rich toward God" (Lk 12:16-21).

Whenever we break the First Commandment – Thou shalt have no other gods before Me – we have trouble approaching God. At some point, things begin to own us as we tie our souls to them. I heard about a young man who was carefree and happy until he inherited great wealth. Instead of enjoying his inheritance, he began to worry about losing it. He spent his days watching the stock market and selling and buying stocks here and there. A significant downturn in the market would send him into panic and then depression. The stress of managing his estate was clearly making his life miserable, but he felt he had no alternative but to do it. He had become a slave to his own wealth.

The only way to defeat materialism is to supersede it by finding something much better - fulfillment in Jesus Christ! As a result, material possessions often lose their appeal and seem so empty and lifeless. They are such a bother to keep up and maintain. I remember thinking it would be nice to own a beach house. But when I eventually spoke with a person who owned one, he recited a list of headaches associated with ownership and maintenance. I have since been cured of that desire.

God already knows what we need. In order to receive help from heaven, we must drop our incessant requirement to have things and instead, require an intimate relationship with God, who created all things.

Let us pray: *Lord Jesus, I see now that things have possessed me and not the other way around. I pray You break their grip on my soul. May Your fulfillment in my heart supersede anything else I'm tempted to worship. May I wait before You in the morning each day until I sense Your sacred presence. Thank You Lord Jesus for being my fulfillment! Amen.*

Freedom from Impatience

Impatience is the inability to defer gratification. We want it now! Deep inside, we know that impatience is a form of selfishness. We also find that help from heaven is seldom given on a schedule that suits us. We cannot wait on God's timing because He seems to be late more than early. After all, Jesus waited four days before going to raise Lazarus from the dead. His sisters wanted to know why Jesus didn't get there sooner to prevent his death.

The great patriarch, Abraham, had trouble waiting on the promise from God that he would become a great nation. Abraham and Sarah had waited 10 years. But there was no child. As they were not getting any younger, they decided to "help" God fulfill His promise. Abraham took his servant woman, Hagar, and had intercourse with her and she conceived a son, Ishmael. The child of promise, Isaac, did not come for another 14 years. The world conflict between Muslims and Jews can be traced back to this set of events. Abraham was impatient with God.

Obviously, that is an extreme case with global significance. But what about the promises God has made to you? Have you waited patiently for those? Some people think God won't come through with a marriage partner, so they hurry the process. They break God's commands about chastity before marriage and end up with someone that is less than ideal. Then they gripe at God because their marriage stinks. In other cases, people don't wait to spend their money wisely because they feel they need the new product or service "right now." Salespeople thrive on our impatience (impulse buying) because it is a moral weakness.

True progress takes time. When I needed help from heaven the most, it did not come that day. Or the next, or the next. It took months. In the meantime, I had to resolve that I would never quit and never give up banging on the gates of heaven. The idea that I may have to tie a knot in my rope and hang on forever if need be, was critical to overcoming impatience. Forever is a long time! But remember, we will spend this time doing something. Why not seek God's kingdom and His righteousness while we are waiting?

Let us pray: *Lord Jesus, I have trouble with impatience. My natural mind cannot stand to wait. So I ask You to let me experience Your supernatural peace and soothing love. I confess that I have placed the wrong priorities on my busy schedule. Because You are my only hope in this life and in the next, may I resolve that no matter how long it takes, I will enjoy my time waiting on You. Amen.*

The Grace of God that Overcomes Obstacles

To most Christians, the definition of grace is the unearned love and mercy we get from God. God's grace is also associated with salvation or forgiveness of sin. But few Christians understand that the Bible speaks of grace as God's power in our lives to overcome the obstacle of sin. Too many Christians are trying to lead good, holy lives on their own without the grace of God. This is a totally impossible task. They are not appropriating this inner power of God's grace by faith. The Bible says that we are saved by grace through faith (Eph 2:8).

The recurring theme in this section about overcoming obstacles is the dependence on God for the cure rather than our independent efforts. The exercise of our faith in this process - believing God can and will fix my problems or empower me to overcome them - is key to victory. If you are like me, you may think you have already tried that method and found it lacking. But I would urge you to give this a second look.

In my original attempts, I was using *my* faith and trying to be good rather than the *gift* of grace that God gives *through* faith. I had faith in my faith rather than faith in God's gift of grace to me - if that makes sense to you. What is the difference between the two? It is the difference between success and failure. My version of "good" and God's version are light years apart. I once thought that God supported my version of "good." But the good that I try to do on my own falls short of God's perfection and lacks all power to overcome sin. I have to remind myself over and over that I serve God and not vice versa. He is the source of everything good and His grace is the power to make me good, as well.

Let us pray: *Heavenly Father, thank You so much for Your grace and the power to overcome my inner sin. I often try to take Your job away from You and do it myself, but it never works. I am always dependent on your loving and merciful heart. I pray right now for more and more of Your grace to overcome my failures and repeated sins. You know my weaknesses. Please strengthen me inwardly with Your magnificent grace. May everything that comes from Your action in me, serve to glorify You. Amen.*

Part 5 – God Prepares Everything

There are stages in spiritual development. When we first come to Christ, we are overjoyed in His forgiveness of our sin, His love, and His acceptance. At that point, He is an addition to our spiritual tool box. As we go on, we find that He is more than just an addition. Rather, He begins to dwarf the other tools in the box. Finally, we learn that He is the box, the tools, and the entirety of our lives. He has quietly prepared everything while we were distracted by our own efforts for a better life. Much of the time, we have tried to do for ourselves the things only God can do.

The Parable of the Wedding Banquet

Jesus told a parable to the people that explained how God provides everything for us, no matter what our previous circumstances or moral standing has been. The parable of the wedding banquet is found in the 22nd chapter of Matthew. In the story, Jesus tells about a king who was preparing a wedding banquet for his son. He invited guests, but they refused to come. He sent servants out to the invited guests to tell them everything was ready – the oxen and fattened cattle had been butchered, all was prepared. The guests did not have to bring anything with them to the wedding feast. Yet even then, the people did not come. In fact, they not only ignored the invitation, some of the invited guests seized the messengers and mistreated and even killed them.

Let me stop here and ask, what is going on? Why would invited guests kill the servants of the king, when all the servants did was to invite the people to a wedding banquet? In the story, it says one went off to his field, the other to his business. In other words, they did not want to be bothered with the king's agenda. They had their own lives to live and their own businesses to attend. But again, why kill the servants of the king? Those annoying witnesses of the king's invitation were put to death because the people were rebelling against all the king represented. As a result, the king sent his army to destroy those rebels who refused to come to his son's wedding banquet.

"Then he said to his servants, 'The wedding banquet is ready, but those I invited did not deserve to come. Go to the street corners and invite to the banquet anyone you find.' So the servants went out into the streets and gathered all the people they could find, both good and bad, and the wedding hall was filled with guests. But when the king came in to see the guests, he noticed a man there who was not wearing wedding clothes. 'Friend,' he asked, 'how did you get in here without wedding clothes?' The man was speechless. Then the king told the attendants, 'Tie him hand and foot, and throw him outside, into the darkness, where there will be weeping and gnashing of teeth'" (Mt 22:8-13).

This episode about the king inviting the good and the bad to the banquet is understandable when we consider the original invited guests did not show up. When Jesus told the story, He may have referred to Jews as the first group versus Gentiles as the second. However, the part about the guest without wedding clothes seems to be a weird ending to the story. It took me years to understand, but this is what I would like you to notice: all was prepared for the guests by the king. All of the food, all of the entertainment, and even the clothing the guests were to wear was prepared and waiting. The guests only had to come and put on the wedding clothes and attend the feast. But one man was found in the banquet without the proper clothing. He had entered the feast without the provided clothes. This ungrateful negligence caused the harsh reaction of the king. That fellow was thrown outside into darkness and misery.

Of course, this is a picture of heaven. The King is God, and His Son is Jesus. But what is the proper clothing? Why are wedding clothes needed? They represent the righteousness of Christ we are to put on. Even when Adam and Eve recognized their nakedness and sin, God provided clothing. (Gn 3:21). Because no sin will be permitted in heaven, God has arranged for our clothing in the righteousness of Christ. "For all of you who were baptized into Christ have clothed yourselves with Christ" (Gal 3:27). In the parable, the guest was wearing his own dirty clothes and could not be admitted into heaven. He may have even thought he was clean. But we cannot clean ourselves to the perfect standard that God requires.

God Himself has resolved every possible problem for our entry into His presence. He has seen to it that we not only have the fattened cattle – food to eat – but also the righteousness of Christ to wear. It's only when we try to do these things for ourselves without Him that we run into trouble. Again, help from heaven requires we include Christ in everything. God is taking us on a journey to perfection. We need to relax, trust God to provide all that is needed, and enjoy the trip!

Let us pray: *Lord Jesus, I often try to do things apart from You. Please help me to see that my enjoyment of these things can be deepened when You are present. Please forgive my foolish ways and create in me a desire to share everything with You. I trust You in preparing all that is needed for me to live the way You want me to live. Thank you for this, Jesus. Amen.*

God's Initiative

Let me follow up on this last thought. If we truly desire help from heaven, we need to consider what God has promised to do for us. Instead of worrying about how we are going to provide for ourselves or grow in our spiritual walk with God, we need to believe that God is more concerned about it than we are. From the following Scripture verses, please tell me which job is God's work and which is ours: "*I will* give you a new heart and put a new spirit in you; *I will* remove from you your heart of stone and give you a heart of flesh. And *I will* put my Spirit in you and move you to follow my decrees and be careful to keep my laws" (Ez 36:26-27, emphasis added). Someone pointed out that in this declaration, God says "I will" three times. He never says "we will" or "you will."

When we don't believe the all-provision of God, many of us have a vague sense that God is disappointed with us. We have heard sermons on the fact that He isn't mad at us because of the work of Jesus, but we still don't believe we have measured up. This feeling dogs many Christians because they live in works-oriented religion. They feel they must make up for their sin by living right and doing good things. The heart of this type of religion is a distrust of the Gospel, which proclaims our forgiveness because of the love of God in Christ Jesus rather than because of our attempts to be good. We simply cannot earn the love of God. We know it, but we don't know it. Dear Christian, God is pleased with you! He knew what He was getting when He saved you.

There are numerous Bible passages where God says He will do a work within us where we have no other role except to receive the gift. "For it is by grace you have been saved, through faith - and this not from yourselves, it is the gift of God - not by works, so that no one can boast. For we are God's workmanship, created in Christ Jesus to do good works, which God prepared in advance for us to do" (Eph 2:8-10). The message is pounded into us that God is doing the work and this is not from ourselves. Further, God has prepared good works for us in advance. He has a plan. Our job is to believe Him.

If we will enter God's presence and wait on Him in faith, expecting and praying for God's sovereign move of grace, we will experience His blessing. Think deeply about this: God has already prepared everything you need. This is not just for super-Christians. It is a promise from God for every believer, weak or strong. Don't worry that you haven't measured up. Quit holding out an impossible standard to live up to as the payment for help from heaven. From the Scripture texts, you can see that our effort is not what achieves the gift. God's free grace brings it about.

If I were you, I would pray for this great generosity of God to occur more quickly in your life, because that's what I pray for myself. Let's stop thinking small and being limited by our own estimation of what God is doing. Let's stop using our shortcomings to limit God.

Let us pray: *Dear Lord Jesus, please help me understand Your plan for my life. I want the whole thing! Forgive me for limiting You in my mind. I have consistently underestimated Your attention to details, Your power, Your goodness, and Your love for me. May I not be satisfied with anything less than Your best for me from heaven. I ask for this in Your name with Your blessing. Amen.*

The Lord Will Keep You

The Bible says repeatedly that the Lord not only saves us, but He will keep us morally clean by His grace. We are so used to trying to keep ourselves clean we overlook this aspect of faith. The apostle Paul wrote of God: "He will keep you strong to the end, so that you will be blameless on the day of our Lord Jesus Christ" (1 Cor 1:8). What does it mean that God will "keep you strong to the end?" I believe that this does not mean physically strong, but instead, spiritually and morally strong because he uses the word "blameless."

I don't know about you, but I have great faith in God. However, I don't have the same great faith in myself, because I know how weak I am and how susceptible to temptation I can be. In fact, it is an impossible task for me to keep myself blameless or sinless until Jesus comes back. I *know* that I cannot do it. But my great hope and my great faith in God's Word is that He will keep me, providing help from heaven to do it.

And yet, many Christians fall into addictions, adulterous relationships, or some type of alienation from God. Thinking back, they realize they have ended up doing just the thing they thought they would never do. How could good intentions backfire so radically? We must face the fact that no amount of human "trying" can overcome the sin that lives within us. If we are trying to be good on our own, we are competing with God. In this case, God is obligated to make us fail; else, we would think our moral excellence was as great as His. If we are going to succeed, God must get the glory.

How Will God Keep You?

Psalm 121 is a great Word to all believers who worry about the future and whether or not they can keep themselves safe, fed, pure, and good enough to get into heaven. This psalm makes it clear that God is the One who keeps us. "I lift up my eyes to the hills - where does my help come from? My help comes from the LORD, the Maker of heaven and earth. He will not let your foot slip - he who watches over you will not slumber; indeed, he who watches over Israel will neither slumber nor sleep. The LORD watches over you - the LORD is your shade at your right hand; the sun will not harm you by day, nor the moon by night. The LORD will keep you from all harm - he will watch over your life; the LORD will watch over your coming and going both now and forevermore" (Ps 121:1-8). If you are tempted to go to sleep mentally when you read this, I would urge you to rouse yourself and take a closer look.

First, the psalmist asks a question that you and I should ask: Where does our help come from? We often seek help from friends, family, doctors, or even the government. The advice of the psalmist is to look upward to our heavenly Father whenever we need help. All of the help we get through people originated in God. So why not go to the Source?

The rest of the psalm gives a picture of God that many Christians don't really believe. Many don't believe God is involved in the tiny details of our lives. They think we call upon Him from across the universe. He arrives and must be brought up to speed on our problems and then figure out an answer for them. The psalmist says just the opposite. He describes God as a Being who watches over His people 24/7, making sure that even their feet don't slip. Several times, the point is made that He is watching over our lives and that watchfulness will keep us from harm.

Like Mary and Martha of the Bible, (Jn 11), many Christians believe if God really were going to keep them from harm, He would have prevented the trouble from happening in the first place. We hear people ask, how could God have allowed the automobile accident, the cancer, the divorce, the bankruptcy, and so on? They don't see it is God Who gives the strength and grace to endure and to go *through* the problem.

Most of us haven't taken God up on His terms, surrendering all and practicing obedience to Him. We haven't believed that God should watch our every move, every thought, and every motivation. If we were honest, many of us would confess we don't want God this close because our motives are impure. We don't want to obey His every command. We've settled for less than God's way and now we don't feel comfortable to have Him watching all we do. It is no wonder there are so many dissatisfied Christians whose prayer life is weak and their joy in the Lord is non-existent.

Here is a challenge for you: believe that no matter what happens, God is looking out for your best life. He never wants to take things away from you unless that will help you in the long run. If you will believe that God's purposes in your life are good, even if they seem bad at the time, you will get your spiritual breakthrough and help from heaven will flow to you in abundance. Let's really believe that God will provide everything necessary to make us blameless before Him.

Let us pray: *Lord Jesus, I thank You and praise You for Your gracious atonement for my sin. Let me experience fully the cure of my internal unrighteousness Your blood purchased for me. May I share that with others as You guide me. I believe You have provided everything I need to keep me blameless in Your sight. Please strengthen this faith in Your grace so that I believe even when circumstances around me appear contrary to Your Word. Amen.*

Trusting God to Cleanse Us

Before I really understood the principles of faith (and even afterwards), I tried to do the work inside my heart that only God can do. I read the Bible; I prayed. Once, I fasted for more than three weeks. But in the end, I had to give up and believe that God, and God alone, could do what needed to be done inside my heart. When Peter told Jesus it was inappropriate for Him to wash his feet, Jesus responded: "Unless I wash you, you have no part with me" (Jn 13:8). Jesus was saying to Peter, and to us, that we cannot clean ourselves. He must do it with our willing faith in His ability to get it done.

God has said, "Never will I leave you; never will I forsake you" (Heb 13:5b). The Amplified Bible puts it this way: "for He [God] Himself has said, I will not in any way fail you nor give you up nor leave you without support. I will not, I will not, I will not in any degree leave you helpless nor forsake nor let you down (relax my hold on you)! Assuredly not!" In the Greek, there are three negatives before the verb "forsake." That is the superlative degree. God is trying to make a point with us to trust Him. Trust Him for what? That He will not leave us in our own strength to be good. What assurance for a weak person like me!

The writer of Hebrews says that we are to fully expected God to equip us for spiritual work. We do not have to climb a mountain in Tibet to visit an enlightened spiritual master in a monastery there. We do not have to translate the Dead Sea Scrolls. We do not have to be "religious" in following rules and regulations. We do not have to get in the mood for spiritual things. We don't even need to use religious Old English with its "thee" and "thou" language in addressing God.

Do we believe that God is working in us, accomplishing all that is pleasing to Him? Do we really believe it? Or are we trying and trying and trying so hard on our own to be the person that God wants us to be? All of our "trying" instead of "believing" will cause us to end up missing the mark. No amount of prayer, Bible reading, or community service seems to work in overcoming some of our internal failures and sinful tendencies.

Unfortunately, this is the state of many Christians today. They are busy trying to do God's job of keeping themselves holy and clean, only to meet with failure. When they fail, their faith is weakened and they begin to doubt the whole Christian life. They haven't learned to trust God to keep them and equip them from the inside out. Their trust was in themselves to do this holy task.

Keeping Us Clean

"He will keep you strong to the end, so that you will be blameless on the day of our Lord Jesus Christ. God, who has called you into fellowship with his Son Jesus Christ our Lord, is faithful" (1 Cor 1:8-9). When the Bible says He (referring to Jesus Christ) will keep you strong to the end, this promise is for those that don't think they have the moral strength to keep themselves blameless for any length of time. God is faithful to do this. Our job is to go into God's presence and *be willing* to believe and trust that He has the power to keep us blameless one day at a time until the end.

There is another Bible passage that underscores the fact that God will keep us clean. "To him who is able to keep you from falling and to present you before his glorious presence without fault and with great joy - to the only God our Savior be glory, majesty, power and authority, through Jesus Christ our Lord, before all ages, now and forevermore! Amen" (Jude 24-25). In these Bible verses, Jude explains God's ability to keep us from falling and to bring us into His glorious presence without fault and with great joy.

Let me ask you, do you feel that you currently have no faults and that you are immune to falling? Are you experiencing life with a joyous heart? Are you able to go into God's glorious presence whenever you desire? How can this be promised to Christians who daily experience falling, faults, and depression? And how about those Christians who are afraid to go into God's presence? Is there a mistake in this grandiose promise?

No! God will do what He has promised to do. This life is available to those who believe it is available. But we need to add our faith to this incredible offer from heaven. The writer of Hebrews pointed this out about the rebellious Israelites in the desert, "For we also have had the gospel preached to us, just as they did; but the message they heard was of no value to them, because those who heard did not combine it with faith" (Heb 4:2).

As you can see, I have tried to say the same thing several different ways: God will keep us clean if we trust Him to do it! Our faith in God's ability to do what we cannot do is vital to receiving this help from heaven.

Please pray with me: *"Lord Jesus, I want to trust You completely with my life. But I don't always do this. I know deep in my heart You love me and have the best plan for my life. Please give me the faith and courage to always trust Your never-failing love. Please take me into Your presence and do the cleansing work that only You can do in my heart. Keep me from betraying You when things don't go well, and make me into the person You created me to be. I ask this in Your name. Amen."*

God Can Help Control Our Words

We often say things in unbelief and thereby undermine God's help from heaven in fulfilling our prayers. For example, if we have a difficult marriage and we pray about it and then complain to a friend about all of our problems, we jeopardize our help from heaven. Likewise, we cannot think bad thoughts about someone and at the same time try to have a good relationship with them. In short, we cannot contradict our prayers with bad thoughts or words and expect good results.

"The tongue also is a fire, a world of evil among the parts of the body. It corrupts the whole person, sets the whole course of his life on fire, and is itself set on fire by hell" (Jas 3:6). Of course, James uses the word "tongue" to mean words or speech. His take on this is extreme. If we don't control our words, it sets our lives on fire, corrupting our entire being!

I know that God is omnipotent, omniscient, and omnipresent. I know that His creation is complex beyond description. I know that the information contained in the human genome is so intricate that it contains over three billion base pairs. I know that God is spinning new galaxies into existence and that He commands great forces. But somehow, this didn't translate into knowing He could pick specific words for me to speak.

Jesus said, "For I did not speak of my own accord, but the Father who sent me commanded me what to say and how to say it" (Jn 12:49). God told Jesus what to say and exactly how to say it. We too can submit our tongues to God and let Him control our words. So why haven't we all done this already? Well it's easy. To avoid moral responsibility, we pretend that we can't hear what God is saying to us.

"For out of the overflow of the heart the mouth speaks" (Mt 12:34b). The real problem with controlling our words is in our hearts. Until God fixes our hearts, we will not speak His language. The good news is that we can be fixed. With Jesus living in our hearts, His ability to hear perfectly from His Father becomes our ability. We can say what God wants us to say and how He wants us to say it. "Wait a minute," you say. "Didn't Jesus tick off the Jewish religious leaders by what He said and get Himself killed?" Yes, He did. But if you remember, He was right in the middle of God's will, "that Scripture be fulfilled." Jesus said, "Whenever you are arrested and brought to trial, do not worry beforehand about what to say. Just say whatever is given you at the time, for it is not you speaking, but the Holy Spirit" (Mk 13:11).

Wow! Do we have to wait until we are put on trial to trust God for our words? Not really - every day can be a trial! Why not take Jesus up on this *before* we get into trouble? If we truly want help from heaven, we have to trust that God has a plan for us; that the plan is perfect; and that we can know this plan. God is faithful on His end and will do what He promises. The Holy Spirit will provide the words we need to survive and thrive in our daily lives! God will help us say the right things!

Let us pray: *Holy Spirit of God, I ask You to tame my heart so that my tongue follows Your lead. Implant Your words and thoughts in me. I believe You control Your creation completely. Please align my will with Yours. May Your grace flow through me to reach this dying world for Jesus. Let the words of my mouth and the meditations of my heart be always acceptable to You. Amen.*

God Controls the Future

Do you believe beyond any doubt that God controls the future? There are times in my life when I have believed just the opposite - that the world was out of control. It seemed like a runaway train hurtling toward a washed out trestle. However, the more I have believed the Bible, the more I see that God is in control of all that happens. Some don't believe that a good God would condone evil. But that is a shallow understanding of reality.

God is not evil, but He does permit evil to exist in order to bring about His good purposes. Perhaps one of the greatest statements of God's provident control of the future was spoken by Joseph of the Old Testament. As you may remember, Joseph's brothers sold him into slavery and treated him very badly. Joseph never lost His faith and when he met his brothers again, (this time as second in command of Egypt) he said, "You intended to harm me, but God intended it for good to accomplish what is now being done, the saving of many lives" (Gn 50:20).

If God doesn't control the future, then praying about the future is in vain. He will not be able to help. Is that your God? Maybe you think He can influence the future, but only to push some events one way or the other. If He can impact some events, why not all events? Do you see that a god who cannot control the future is no God at all, but a toothless inventor who has no power over his creation?

God is in control and we need to deal with it. At one time, that statement made me feel uncomfortable. I thought it meant I was like some robot going through preplanned motions of life. I rebelled against that concept and tried to run my own life. When it fell apart, I had to repent and seek the very God I had rejected. I found I would never be happy until I could revere and accept God's provision for everything in my life. This did not excuse me from work. I must do my best, but I must leave the rest to God.

Our buy-in to His provision is the only way to ensure happiness and joy in this life and the life after death. Abiding in Christ by faith and trust takes the worry out of the future and assures us of help from heaven each day as we need it.

Let us pray: *Lord Jesus, I thank You that Your plan is so big I can't see the beginning or ending of it. I have worried long enough about providing for myself! I trust You to provide the things I need. I will do my best, but trust You for the rest. I believe Your plan is good and that I am right in the middle of it. Please increase my faith in You - not just for the here and now, but for all eternity. I love You, Lord. Praise be to You! Amen.*

Part 6 - Faith

Without faith, it is impossible to please God (Heb 11:6). I want to please God and I'm sure you do too. But we cannot do it without faith. In fact, extraordinary help from heaven is waiting on our faith to ask for it. In this section of the book, we will look at faith and how to increase it. The apostles asked Jesus to increase their faith and so must we.

Negative Faith

Just as there is positive faith, there is negative faith that works as strongly as it is believed. If you expect something bad to happen, you are actually hoping that it will. We don't see it that way, but our negative expectations are a type of faith. I never considered the possibility of negative faith until I witnessed example after example of negative beliefs come true to negative believers. For decades, the University of Kentucky's (UK) football program produced a losing team in the Southeastern Conference. UK fans lost hope of winning and actually came to believe the team would lose most of their games. Once this mindset permeated the fan base, negative faith became ingrained in the team itself and part of its culture. This negative belief helped the team lose game after game in miraculous fashion. Sports headlines would read, "UK Snatches Defeat from the Jaws of Victory."

In one miraculous finish, UK was playing Louisiana State University (LSU) in 2002. At the time, UK was unranked and LSU was ranked 14th in the nation. UK was leading 30 to 27 with two seconds to go. LSU was on its own 26 yard line with the ball. On the last play of the game, the ball was thrown deep and appeared to be touched by at least one UK player and one LSU player. However, another LSU player ended up catching the deflected pass and scoring a touchdown, winning the game. This play is called the "Bluegrass Miracle" and is part of sports lore in Southeastern Conference football. I believe this is an example of negative faith at work. So many people believed UK would find a way to lose that their faith was rewarded with a miracle finish on the part of LSU.

There is the phrase: "What I feared has come upon me; what I dreaded has happened to me" (Job 3:25). This fear and dread is negative faith working against us. We fear something because we secretly believe it will happen to us. We are giving a home to negative faith in our hearts. Yes, on the outside we dread the possible negative consequences. But on the inside, our negative faith is strong – pulling and attracting that bad thing into our lives.

In Jesus' day, they called negative faith, "unbelief." When people believe the opposite of God's positive promises, they are engaged in unbelief. We tend to mix unbelief with belief and get very poor results from our Christian faith. No wonder our prayer lives are weak. No wonder the Church in America has lost strength. It is filled with people who practice negative faith alongside their positive faith.

If we are willing, Jesus can reverse our negative faith. He can empower belief. God can awaken our minds to the choice of positive over negative - belief over unbelief. So don't be deceived into believing you have a bad future or that your life is over because you screwed up badly in the past. Instead, let's be willing to believe the wonderful promises God has made to us in the Bible about our future and His complete forgiveness of our sins.

Let us pray: *Lord Jesus, I catch myself thinking negative thoughts all the time. I know at its root, this is unbelief. I believe You have the best life for me, even if events seem negative at the time. Help me to believe the positive Truth of Your gospel and may it set me free to serve You with my whole heart. I ask this in Your all-powerful name, Amen.*

Faith and Salvation

If our goal is to someday enter heaven, we need to understand that dying is not the only requirement to get in. God has imposed conditions. And the first condition is true repentance for our sin. The Bible makes it clear that no unrepentant sinner will enter heaven. None! Jesus said, "But unless you repent, you too will *all* perish" (Lk 13:5, emphasis added).

The second condition is saving faith – not just mental assent to God's truth. We are saved by grace *through faith* (Eph 2:8). The Bible says: "And without faith it is impossible to please God, because anyone who comes to him must believe that he exists and that he rewards those who earnestly seek him" (Heb 11:6). Those ministers who say God loves you "unconditionally" are not telling the whole truth. There are conditions required on our end and faith is one of them. I've heard it said God loves you just the way you are but He loves you too much to leave you like that.

Jesus talked about faith and our need for it throughout His ministry. He condemned the Jews for not having faith and admonished His disciples for their "little faith." When asked what work God expects of His people, Jesus replied, "The work of God is this: to believe in the one he has sent" (Jn 6:29). As mentioned before, the job of the believer is to *believe*. That is our work!

What are we to believe? We are to believe in Jesus and all His ministry proclaims. Here are some of the faith-building statements Jesus made. He can plant these truths within us by our faith in His indwelling Spirit and power:

- I am the Way, the Truth, and the Life (Jn 14:6)
- No one comes to the Father except through Me (Jn 14:6)
- I am the Vine; you are the branches (Jn 15:5)
- I am the good Shepherd (Jn 10:14)
- Whoever believes in Him (God) shall not perish but have eternal life (Jn 3:16)
- My peace I give you (Jn 14:27)
- Therefore I tell you, do not worry (Mt 6:25)
- It is I; don't be afraid (Mk 6:50)

- Neither do I condemn you. Go now and leave your life of sin (Jn 8:11)
- The Son of Man has authority on earth to forgive sins (Mk 2:10)
- They may receive forgiveness of sins and a place among those who are sanctified by faith in Me (Acts 26:18)
- Anyone who has faith in Me will do what I have been doing (Jn 14:12)
- Receive the Holy Spirit (Jn 20:22)
- When He, the Spirit of Truth, comes, He will guide you into all Truth (Jn 16:13)
- Get behind Me, Satan! (Mt 16:23)

Do you believe these words of Jesus? Can you handle the Truth? By believing, you will receive help from heaven. It can happen in an instant. Let us trust God right now to give us believing faith!

Let us pray: *Lord Jesus, I need strong, believing faith. Please grant me faith and favor with You. I long for closer communion with You and more of Your Holy Spirit within me. Please increase my faith. Lead me and guide me along Your perfect path. Amen.*

Paul and Silas

In demonstrating the practical power of faith and how it releases help from heaven, there is a story in the Bible about the apostle Paul and his fellow teacher Silas. They were ministering in the city of Philippi when the following incident occurred: "This girl followed Paul and the rest of us, shouting, 'These men are servants of the Most High God, who are telling you the way to be saved.' She kept this up for many days. Finally Paul became so troubled that he turned around and said to the spirit, 'In the name of Jesus Christ I command you to come out of her!' At that moment the spirit left her" (Acts 16:17-18).

From that time forward, the woman could no longer earn money by predicting the future. So her owners seized Paul and Silas. "They brought them before the magistrates and said, 'These men are Jews, and are throwing our city into an uproar advocating customs unlawful for us Romans to accept or practice.' The crowd joined in the attack against Paul and Silas, and the magistrates ordered them to be stripped and beaten. After they had been severely flogged, they were thrown into prison, and the jailer was commanded to guard them carefully. Upon receiving such orders, he put them in the inner cell and fastened their feet in the stocks. About midnight Paul and Silas were praying and singing hymns to God, and the other prisoners were listening to them. Suddenly there was such a violent earthquake that the foundations of the prison were shaken. At once all the prison doors flew open, and everybody's chains came loose" (Acts 16:20-26).

There are a couple of important details about faith from this story that I would like you to notice. First, Paul and Silas were beaten and severely flogged. Their backs were bleeding and they were placed in stocks so they couldn't move. Yet, what were they doing at midnight? They were praying and singing hymns to God. Not just to themselves, but to the entire prison! Despite the pain, they were taking everything they had to the Lord and praising Him. They didn't blame God for their situation. They believed God was able to minister to them and to rescue them. And that is exactly what happened. God responded to their believing prayers with supernatural actions. There was a violent earthquake and not only did the doors of the prison fly open, everyone's chains came loose.

Just so you don't think this is some type of natural accident, chains don't come loose even during an earthquake. Stocks don't release their prisoners just because they are shaken. God moved directly on their imprisonment and released them.

But there is a second part of the story. "The jailer woke up, and when he saw the prison doors open, he drew his sword and was about to kill himself because he thought the prisoners had escaped. But Paul shouted, 'Don't harm yourself! We are all here!' The jailer called for lights, rushed in and fell trembling before Paul and Silas. He then brought them out and asked, 'Sirs, what must I do to be saved?' They replied, 'Believe in the Lord Jesus, and you will be saved - you and your household.' Then they spoke the word of the Lord to him and to all the others in his house. At that hour of the night the jailer took them and washed their wounds; then immediately he and all his family were baptized" (Acts 16:27-33).

Notice what happened to the jailer and his family. Because Paul and Silas trusted God and received a miracle, the jailer, who was about to kill himself, was saved as well. Paul stopped the man from committing suicide. So he was saved from physical death. But then, the jailer asks, "Sirs, what must I do to be saved?" They gave him the simple answer – believe in the Lord Jesus.

Paul and Silas were not super-Christians because they were made out of better material than you and me. They were super-Christians because they believed firmly in the power of Christ to rescue them out of any circumstance. God gave them help from heaven in response to their faith. You and I can take advantage of this great gift as well. But it must start with our belief that help from heaven will come. God rewards those who have faith that He exists and who earnestly seek Him.

Let us pray: *Lord Jesus, I believe You are instantly accessible to me through my faith and prayers. I am believing that You will work through the faith You have given me to reach others with the good news of Your gospel. Please strengthen my resolve to never quit and never give up believing in Your ultimate victory here on earth, and within me, personally. I ask this in Your blessed name, Amen.*

Faith and Confidence

"Dear friends, if our hearts do not condemn us, we have confidence before God and receive from him anything we ask, because we obey his commands and do what pleases him" (1 Jn 3:21-22). Are there Christians today that receive everything for which they ask? Do you? Most Christians do not experience this type of help from heaven and if they were honest, they would tell you they lack confidence before God. They know they have failed to keep God's commandments and the guilt of their disobedience keeps them from feeling confident before Him.

A key phrase is "if our hearts do not condemn us." Our consciences must be clean to have the internal confidence to pray with real faith, because confidence and faith are joined at the hip. The apostle Paul understood the need for a clear conscience when he said: "So I strive always to keep my conscience clear before God and man" (Acts 24:16). He also said: "By rejecting and thrusting from them [their conscience], some individuals have made shipwreck of their faith" (1 Tm 1:19b AMP).

With a clear conscience, we feel free to ask favors from God. We don't mind hanging out with Him. We can persevere with God in prayer because we have no reason to think He will deny our requests. On the other hand, a guilty conscience makes us act like Adam and Eve - we run and hide from God. We can't get help from heaven if we are hiding from God and ashamed of ourselves.

So how do we get clean consciences, particularly when we fail and continue to sin? The only way is to believe the promises of God in the Bible. Do you believe this Scripture verse: "If we confess our sins, he is faithful and just and will forgive us our sins and purify us from all unrighteousness" (1 Jn 1:9)? This statement is true whether or not we *feel* it. When we don't feel forgiven, it doesn't mean that we aren't actually forgiven. Some of us need to repent and confess our sins so we can be purified from them. Believing that Jesus paid the penalty of all our sins will help our feelings catch up to our actual state of cleanliness before God. When we feel clean before God, our confidence returns.

The Bible helps us to overcome our feelings of insecurity before God by telling us the truth about the forgiveness available through Jesus Christ. He is not against me in my quest for righteousness. In fact, He is the only way I can become righteous and have a clear conscience before the holiness of God. Now when I sin, rather than run and hide, I try to get even closer to the only One who can heal my brokenness and restore my confidence. Through Christ, I know help from heaven is available!

Let us pray: *Dear Lord Jesus, thank You for loving me first! I repent for my sin and confess it to You now. (Pause and reflect). May I always run to You to heal my brokenness and restore my faith. May my confidence in Your Word grow as I believe the Truth. I ask this in Your holy name. Amen.*

Faith Cures Blindness

In a certain sense, obstacles to receiving help from heaven are caused by our own blindness to the illuminating light of God. And as dastardly as it sounds, we have an enemy who is working to keep us blinded.

The Amplified Bible says, "For the god of this world has blinded the unbelievers' minds that they should not discern the truth, preventing them from seeing the illuminating light of the Gospel of the glory of Christ (the Messiah), Who is the Image and Likeness of God" (2 Cor 4:4 AMP). The "god of this world" refers to Satan. Notice, however, that it is the *unbelievers'* minds that are blinded, not the *believers'* minds.

The old hymn, *Amazing Grace*, has a line that reads, "I once was blind, but now I see." What caused the new ability to see? It was the amazing grace. But how did the person receive that grace? The hymn explains: "How precious did that grace appear, the hour I first believed." This hymn relates the true story of a slave trader named John Newton who converted to Christianity. And it records the fact that heavenly grace appeared when he first believed. That is when his spiritual blindness left him.

You have heard that "blind faith" is sometimes considered a virtue. But our faith is not blind. Letting go of our future and placing it in the Lord's care is not a blind act of faith. It is an action based upon reason, historical evidence, and trust in the power of Christ's love for us. The world says, "seeing is believing." But we say, "believing is seeing." Spiritual blindness is cured by faith.

You and I cannot control the future of this world or add a single day to our lives. All rests in God's care. Instead of fighting with it, let us resolve to believe God's promises about our future with Him. He cares for us down to the very hairs on our heads. One day, we will stand before Him without any ability to blind ourselves to His reality. Why not trust Him completely before that time?

Let us pray: *Dear Lord Jesus, I trust You with my life. Yes, I trust my life to You. I thank You for giving me the faith I need to cure my spiritual blindness. Please increase my faith. No matter what the future brings, I know that I am safe with You. Thank You for giving me Your heavenly vision. Amen.*

Jesus Made It Clear

Every believer in Jesus has access to help from heaven. Jesus said, "I tell you the truth, anyone who has faith in me will do what I have been doing. He will do even greater things than these, because I am going to the Father. And I will do whatever you ask in my name, so that the Son may bring glory to the Father. You may ask me for anything in my name, and I will do it" (Jn 14:12-14). This statement is often discounted because we don't believe it applies to us.

In John 15, Jesus repeated it: "If you remain in me and my words remain in you, ask whatever you wish, and it will be given you" (Jn 15:7). Again, in John 16 He hammered the point home to His disciples: "In that day you will no longer ask me anything. I tell you the truth, my Father will give you whatever you ask in my name" (Jn 16:23). On the night before His death, Jesus repeated this promise three times to make sure His disciples understood. By faith, this promise of help from heaven applies to you and me.

So why doesn't this work for many Christians? In many cases, they are using "in the name of Jesus" as an incantation for producing magical results. Remember, Jesus said that we must remain in Him. The power of answered prayer comes from Jesus, not from the prayer itself. To really ask God for something in the name of Jesus, we need to live in Him and He in us. He is the power.

What if we waited each morning in very presence of Jesus, praying until we felt His strength coursing through our veins? How would our days be different? Instead, many of us charge out and throw up a quick prayer that Jesus give us strength to face the schedule we have created for ourselves. We may not have consulted Him about it, but when things get tough, we are looking for Jesus, asking Him to bail us out and to bless our efforts.

We have it backwards. We are not following Jesus. We have asked Jesus to follow us. No. The time to seek the presence of the Lord is before we set the schedule, before we set priorities, and before we commit our time to projects He may not support. Any distraction we face in this is designed by the enemy to keep us from living with constant help from heaven.

Jesus was deadly serious about asking and receiving and He is the one that pointed out why we don't have those results: "Because you have so little faith. I tell you the truth, if you have faith as small as a mustard seed, you can say to this mountain, 'Move from here to there' and it will move. Nothing will be impossible for you" (Mt 17:20). We think these statements are spiritual hyperbole. But why not take Jesus up on them? Our lack of faith in the power of Jesus within us separates us from the abundant living He spoke about. This is not a name it, claim it religion. And I am not speaking about material wealth. I am talking about the promises in the Bible that are available to fully surrendered believers in the King of heaven who graciously lives within them.

Let us pray: *Dear Lord Jesus, I confess I have not believed Your words fully. I have weakened them with my unbelief. Help me to believe completely in You! Help me to live the full life of faith that You have prepared for me. May You be glorified through all that I do and say today. Amen.*

The Test Before the Promotion

Our faith will always be tested before our promotion. Similar to school, we cannot be promoted to the next level of spiritual breakthrough until we pass the test God has designed specifically for us. These tests occur in real life and God will often use methods we do not expect. Our defenses may be focused on protecting a certain vulnerable point in our persona. However, God ignores that route and selects something we thought was off-limits for any testing.

For example, a friend told me about his testing. He was praying that his faith in God become stronger and that his finances improve. He wanted his marriage to get better and his career to advance. Instead, just the opposite occurred. His career suffered, his finances went south, the IRS cleaned out his bank account, his wife had an affair and then divorced him. Up until this point, this man had been a strong Christian in his own right. He was always the cheerful one, always ready to pray for others. In his dark night of the soul, this man made a decision to trust God. Much of his former strength in the Lord came from his strong personality, but with each successive blow, that strength was reduced to nothing.

His complete trust in God ultimately came during his weakness, not his strength. God's answer to his prayer was not in the manner he was expecting. When he surrendered completely to God and trusted his life to Him, he could pray earnestly for his unfaithful wife. He could rely on the Lord's provision, no matter what his finances were. Through this entire process, he told me he had never been closer to the Lord and though it was very painful, he would do it all again to gain that closeness with God.

Our testing, it turns out, is often between our love of God and our love of comfort. Christians outside America perceive the Church in America is very weak. They believe it needs persecution in order to become strong. And it is true that until our very lives depend upon our faith, we cannot know how strong it is. There is something about pain and suffering that separates us from anything synthetic as we seek relief in the Lord. When in pain, we tend to jettison everything except that which is most important to us. At some point, we get down to just God. And that is enough.

The Bible asserts repeatedly that God uses suffering to increase our faith. This suffering is not something that we can set up for ourselves to strengthen our faith. God must do it and we must not question God's goodness when He does. Our job is to get closer to Him during our trouble, and that incredible desire for closeness is part of the definition of faith. It is a felt need that cannot come to us in our comfort until after we have passed the test.

Because suffering is unavoidable in this life, why not turn that around and deliberately seek to enjoy the test? The Bible urges us to "Consider it pure joy, my brothers, whenever you face trials of many kinds, because you know that the testing of your faith develops perseverance." (Jas 1:2-3). Pure joy? Why? Testing develops perseverance in us and when we persevere, we can finish the testing process and get all that God wants us to get out of it. The only way you can lose is to quit. There is an incredible blessing waiting for those willing to undergo God's testing. So don't be afraid to ask for it in prayer. When we really have to trust God under hard circumstances, it bonds us with Him. That is our reward for passing the test!

Let us pray: *Dear Lord Jesus, I have been afraid of tests that may actually strengthen my faith. Help me to trust You so thoroughly, that whatever You do for my good — painful or not - I am willing to look at with a grateful attitude. May I consider it pure joy when I am tested. Help me to get to the point where I seek You earnestly before these things happen to me. Let me enter Your presence daily and live according to Your Word, for I ask this in Your holy name. Amen.*

Learning Never Stops

In spiritual terms, we have never arrived or graduated if we are still alive. Many people make the mistake of thinking their initial encounter with Jesus is something to put behind them as they get back on their feet and begin their new life as Christians. They believe being "saved" or "born again" through Jesus was the whole goal of their religious experience. They hope to move beyond this vulnerable stage and back to some type of self-reliance that permitted them to survive in their pre-Jesus world.

But our complete dependence on Jesus is the point of being saved. We are not to grow out of that dependent relationship. Yes, we will mature in our faith. And yes, our experience with Jesus will change. But instead of becoming independent of Him, our faith should be aimed at getting closer and becoming more obedient and reliant on Him. The apostle Paul recognized when he was weak, he was strong in Christ.

Typically, new Christians find Jesus is their strength and they can call upon Him to slay the dragons that have stood in their way. They quote the Scripture: "I can do all things through Christ which strengtheneth me" (Phil 4:13 KJV), and use that in their battle charge. After a while, however, they find their newfound strength fails them and that many of the problems Jesus was taking care of come back. They may question their faith and think they just didn't believe hard enough or keep God's commands perfectly enough for Jesus to stay around and continue to fix the problems. So they redouble their efforts - they pray more, do more Bible study and church work. But this doesn't help. Their new faith has taken a hit and they are left with doubt and questions about whether or not they really were converted or are qualified to receive help from heaven.

If this describes your experience, you are not alone. Many Christians make the mistake of thinking they must add Jesus as a tool in their bag of tricks to engage the world. Rather than change their approach to life, they have a new Weapon to work their old plan. However, in most cases, Jesus is not calling us to overcome our problems the same way we did before we met Him. Instead, He is looking for a complete shift of power – one that moves from us to Him.

Simply stated, we need to keep the same humility, brokenness, and gratitude that we had when we first gave our hearts to Jesus. Our weakness allows us to place our faith in Christ alone as our strength. Most of us were grateful that He came and that He touched our darkened hearts with His love. The fresh newness of His touch, the life-altering contact in our spirits, and the newfound ability to resist the old temptations came with our spiritual rebirth. We depended on Him for everything. Only later did we feel the need to leave this cozy relationship and strike out on our own for God. Just when we should be spending time in His presence, waiting on Him, and absorbing the radiance of His being, we leave on a mission for Him. Most of the time this mission is conducted with good intentions; but in our own strength rather than His.

He is the power, not us. He can overcome any obstacle, but you and I are the first ones He has to conquer. Our desire to run our own lives will kill us. We have to be completely obedient to His voice if we are going to receive help from heaven. That means we have to spend time each day listening to God, waiting in His presence for His power and direction. The advice He gave His disciples applies to us: "Wait for the gift my Father promised, which you have heard me speak about. . . You will receive power when the Holy Spirit comes on you" (Acts 1:4, 8). We are to wait in holy expectation each morning before the face of God. If there is a transaction with the Lord, we will know when His power has come upon us. His power is the help from heaven for which we thirst!

Let us pray: *Dear Lord Jesus, help me to never stop learning about You. Please reset my assumptions about what it means to mature in the faith. May I never grow independent of You. I want to want what You want. I want to see through Your eyes. I want to love with Your love. Please give me the ability to wait on You in the morning until You touch my spirit. Amen.*

Waiting in the Presence of God

Martin Luther said, "I have so much to do that I shall spend the first three hours in prayer." If you want help from heaven, you must cultivate a spirit of waiting in the presence of God that expects Him to supply direction, power, and love to your spirit. Internal impatience makes it tough to wait on anything. "But they that wait upon the LORD shall renew *their* strength; they shall mount up with wings as eagles; they shall run, and not be weary; *and* they shall walk, and not faint" (Is 40:31 KJV). It is interesting that the NIV translation of the Bible changes the word "wait" to the word "hope." While we are waiting we should be hoping and expecting God to move. This is active faith.

Here is the thought of waiting: "As the eyes of a maid look to the hand of her mistress, so our eyes look to the LORD our God, till he shows us his mercy" (Ps 123:2b). Isn't it interesting that they call the staff of restaurants "waiters" and "waitresses?" Their job is to watch patrons closely and respond quickly when summoned. A good waiter will anticipate the need by watching their table of guests.

King David, a man after God's own heart, knew the value of waiting. "In the morning, O LORD, you hear my voice; in the morning I lay my requests before you and wait in expectation" (Ps 5:3). In another psalm, David wrote: "Wait for the LORD; be strong and take heart and wait for the LORD" (Ps 27:14). And again: "I wait for you, O LORD; you will answer, O Lord my God" (Ps 38:15). There is a pattern here. When David had a pressing need, instead of marching out on his own to take care of the problem, he asked for help and then waited for God to move or to give him the answer. David was a man of war and action, but he knew that waiting on God was critical to winning the day.

We too, have daily battles that we must fight. Our battles may not be bloody, but they involve personal struggle. Let's use our faith and wait in the presence of God for His help in these battles! "I wait for the LORD, my soul waits, and in his word I put my hope. My soul waits for the Lord more than watchmen wait for the morning, more than watchmen wait for the morning" (Ps 130:5-6). Andrew Murray pointed out that in ancient times, battles were fought mostly in daylight hours when the enemy could be seen. However, there were times of siege that required nightly watching for the enemy for a surprise attack in darkness. To the watchman, the morning light was desperately needed. That light meant greater safety and knowledge of the enemy's movements. Yet the psalmist says that his soul waited for the Lord *more* than watchmen waited for morning. What great hope! What salvation and rescue is implied!

We are to wait expectantly on the Lord in faith. Jesus commanded us to keep watch for Him (Mt 24:42). To notice His movement, we must be in His presence while we wait. If you are looking for help from heaven, you must keep your spiritual eyes on the Lord of heaven while you wait. Try this. In the morning as you wait on God, ask Him, "How can I serve You today?" and mean it. Think about what it means to take directions from God instead of giving Him requests. Know that it is our highest honor to wait upon and serve the living God.

Let us pray: *Dear Lord Jesus, I bless Your holy name with all of my heart. I ask You to increase my faith in You and Your Word. Teach me to wait in Your presence. May I derive my joy from serving You rather than trying to get things from You in prayer. Please increase my faith. Thank You, Jesus. I praise and worship You. Amen.*

Part 7 - Obedience

Until we have surrendered our lives to Jesus, we cannot trust Him with our obedience. A surrendered life has no agenda of its own. Most of us already know that our best choice is to surrender, but we can't bring ourselves to give up control. We want to work the joystick. We want to choose the time of our obedience. We want to reserve the right to sin when and where it suits us. Because we know better, we are living in disobedience to God. This is what rebellion looks like. Most of us don't even think of this as sin or rebellion. But R.C. Sproul called sin "cosmic treason."

In my old way of trying to obey God, I would consider His commands and then try to summon up the courage to obey those commands. For example, Jesus told us to go into all the world and make disciples out of people and spread the good news of the Gospel. Well, I would check my reservoir of courage and think about whether I could withstand the negative thoughts of people and whether being a follower of Christ would cost me some work or alienate me from people. If I thought it was just too much, I would not even try to do what I knew God would like me to do. That's because I was trying to do God's will in my own strength. It simply cannot be done that way.

The Heavenly Gift from Jesus Helps Us Obey

What is the heavenly gift from Jesus? Most Christians would answer, "Eternal life." Others would answer, "The Holy Spirit." While these answers are not incorrect, there is an immediate gift Jesus gives that is very little appropriated by Christians: a full measure of joy in our hearts. The night before He died, Jesus prayed, "I am coming to you now, but I say these things while I am still in the world, so that they may have the full measure of my joy within them" (Jn 17:13).

When Jesus spoke of giving us His joy, there was a context for receiving it: "As the Father has loved me, so have I loved you. Now remain in my love. If you obey my commands, you will remain in my love, just as I have obeyed my Father's commands and remain in his love. I have told you this so that my joy may be in you and that your joy may be complete" (Jn 15:9-11). There it is! The joy of Jesus was founded in His obedience to God's commands and remaining in His Father's love. Similarly, by obeying the commands of Jesus, we remain in His love and His joy lives inside us.

Joy in Christ makes obedience easy. How many Christians are lacking this ingredient in their lives? We pray. We fast. We go to church, and we listen to Christian music. We do volunteer work. All the while, the joy that Jesus died to give us is only felt sporadically. We are doing superficial Christianity. Where is this constant, full measure of joy? It is no wonder that the Church is weak in America. It is joyless! Our delight is somewhere else.

Jesus prayed about this, saying, "I have made you known to them, and will continue to make you known in order that the love you have for me may be in them and that I myself may be in them" (Jn 17:26). The living love of Jesus is poured into every believer through the Holy Spirit. Jesus speaks about the divine love God has for Him being in you and me. That is the delight and full measure of joy Jesus is talking about. But it does little good if we cannot recognize, feel, and experience its full measure. That love, that peace, that joy which passes all human understanding is our heritage as Christians. We may experience a little of it from time to time. However, there is no reason to leave most of it in heaven.

Our obedience to God's commands reigns from the beginning to the end of the Bible. Jesus made sure we understood this by saying that the only measure of our love for Him was our obedience to His commands.

Even if we think we are too weak and ruled by sin, if we will simply be *willing* to obey in our minds, Christ will do the rest over time.

Let us pray: *Lord Jesus, create in me a willing heart to obey You. Open my ears to hear Your voice. Open my eyes to see Your plan. Help me to know You better and live my life in You rather than apart from You. Thank You for Your intimate care of me and for loving me even when I don't obey You. Amen.*

The Way of Obedience

There is a direct connection between obedience to God and help from heaven. This connection is not there so that we can "work the system" through obedience to get things. Instead, it is a living connection of love. Jesus reminded us several times on the last night of His life on earth: "If you love me, you will obey what I command" (Jn 14:15). He wanted to underline it to His disciples: "If anyone loves me, he will obey my teaching. My Father will love him, and we will come to him and make our home with him. He who does not love me will not obey my teaching" (Jn 14:23-24).

For many years, this command of Jesus did not sink in. I would simply "wing it" on a daily basis. That is, I would approach each day without the goal of obedience to God. I was busy attending to urgent things, but ignoring the direct commands of Jesus. I somehow thought if I were super-observant of His commands, I would be under *legalism* and not free in Christ. But it turns out the difference between legalism and freedom in Christ is our attitude about obedience to Him. If we are compelled to do it by guilt, be assured that legalism is at work. If we desire to obey Jesus out of love, then Christ will expand our perception of His love in us.

The Bible says, "For we are God's workmanship, created in Christ Jesus to do good works, which God prepared in advance for us to do" (Eph 2:10). God has already prepared good works for you and me to do! That is where obedience comes in. We have a plan from heaven! It is the very source of our help. We don't have to invent our own life every day or wonder what obedience looks like. We simply need to love the One who has planned good works for us and then do what He asks us to do.

"Whether you turn to the right or to the left, your ears will hear a voice behind you, saying, 'This is the way; walk in it'" (Is 30:21).

But how do we approach obedience with a good attitude all of the time? Living out a pre-planned life doesn't sound exciting until we add God to the mix. Jesus' life went exactly as planned. Yet it was anything but dull. God's plan for us is voluntary on our part. Jesus said, "*If* anyone would follow me. . ." (Mt 16:24, emphasis added). Jesus prefaced His statement with "if." He is not making us do anything. Out of His great love, that which He tells us to do is for our own benefit.

So in order to conquer my disobedience (or my way of doing things apart from God), I have had to think of it this way: God knows what is best for each of us. Everything we do on our own is harder and creates messes that could have been avoided if only we had listened to God and obeyed His command. Disobedience cannot be overcome by fighting disobedience. It must be overcome by striving positively to obey God. This is similar to the Biblical injunction to overcome evil with good (rather than just fighting evil). God's command is the shortcut through trouble and the surest way to receive help from heaven.

Let us pray: *Lord Jesus, please teach me obedience to You. Let my heart be open to Your guidance daily. I wait in Your presence now to receive direction and energy to accomplish Your will. May this time be blessed, for I ask this in Your name. Amen.*

Love Takes the Work Out of Obedience

C.S. Lewis pointed out that the law of human nature (which some may call our *conscience*) tells us what we ought and ought not to do. When our conscience tells us to do something and we ignore it, we get this gnawing sense of disobedience. How much easier it is to do what we ought to do when we love Jesus! Instead of thinking about the task at hand, we are focused on the love of Christ. He was right! If we love Him, we will obey Him because love takes the "work" out of obedience.

There is a story in the Old Testament about Jacob and Rachel that illustrates this point. "Jacob was in love with Rachel and said, "I'll work for you seven years in return for your younger daughter Rachel." Laban said, "It's better that I give her to you than to some other man. Stay here with me." So Jacob served seven years to get Rachel, but they seemed like only a few days to him because of his love for her" (Gn 29:18-20). Wow! Seven years of work seemed like only a few days to man who was in love. On the other hand, we all know how the seconds seem like hours while we sit in the dentist's chair or begin a task we dislike. Time seems to stand still when the unwanted guest won't leave or the traffic jam grinds our progress to a halt when we are in a hurry.

The secret to enjoying both the good times and the bad times is to do it in the company of Jesus with love. If we love Him, obedience is easy. No task is too hard. No situation is too tough to apply His love and find relief. When I was young, I took a radio with me to work on my outdoor farm jobs. This was my lifeline to the world and my escape from the dullness of the task. Now, I have a much better Lifeline that loves me back and communicates directly to me in answer to prayer. As long as I remember to bring Him along, my day is great! This is how we receive help from heaven to obey Christ. Every minute of every day can be a joyous time because we know the Author of all joy and happiness.

God Is in the Details

Many people think it is sacrilegious to take God into their non-religious lives. Yes, we need God for the big things in life, but we don't want to bother Him with the small stuff. However, He actually wants to advise you on your golf game, your choice of clothing, your reading material, and even what you look at when you are a passenger in a car. We need to realize that all things to God are small things. Our biggest problem is nothing to Him. Don't be like the disciples who told the blind man to be quiet and not bother Jesus. We need to bother Him with everything, because He wants us to live that way (Dt 11:18-19).

It is easier to disobey God when we don't believe He understands the details of our lives. A large part of obedience is believing that God, and not the devil, is in the details. When we view God as a vague "force" or some impersonal power, we deny not just His kingship over our lives, but His involvement in the details of our lives. Many believers of "free will" try to use that belief to limit God and tie His hands so He won't intervene directly in their lives. But instead, we need to unleash God in our minds and give Him the controls if we really want His help from heaven. He is well able to guide our thought processes and our words into the most complex situations.

Think about Moses delivering the law of God to the Israelites. That law has guided Western Civilization for centuries. Every word had to be perfect or it could have taken the culture down a false path. Moses had to be completely obedient to God in his mind in order to complete such a task. And that is why the disobedience of Moses kept him from the Promised Land. Do you remember the reason? It was because Moses struck a rock for water rather than speaking to the rock! Water was produced from the rock after he struck it, but because of that disobedience, Moses only *saw* the Promised Land but was not allowed to *enter* it.

For you and me, the difference between speaking to a rock and striking it may have been just a small error. But for Moses, the man who repeated the law of God to the people exactly as he received it, this action was a grave disobedience. You and I must learn that God wants us to obey Him down to the smallest word He places in our mouths. When we do, we are loving God the way He wants to be loved.

Let us pray: *Lord Jesus, please forgive my disobedience. Since I have awakened this morning, I have not obeyed You completely for more than five minutes. I ask You to give me a love for You and Your commands. Help me to delight in obedience to You. I thank You and ask this in Your holy name and to Your glory. Amen.*

Prayer Enables Obedience

The ability to obey Christ and receive His help from heaven requires we do personal business with Him through much prayer. Carnal Christians (partially committed Christians still mastered by human weakness and desire) have enough of Christ to stay out of hell, but not enough to become joy-filled and worry-free. They must work very hard to maintain any peace of mind, and even then, it is only temporary. They are still taking care of self and have not surrendered all to Jesus in obedience. They have compromised what they know the Holy Spirit is telling them to do.

Prayer is meant to place us in the very presence of God. That is when we can fully absorb His love, light, and joy. But when many of us pray, we go to a lifeless place in our minds where it is quiet and dark. That is the opposite of what God would have us do. Our prayer time should be the most joyous part of our day. When we think about prayer, we should anticipate the wonder of experiencing God's love within the deepest core of our being. There is nothing in our day that can top this one-on-One experience of love!

When I used to *think* about spiritual things, I confused this with praying. I figured that God was reading my thoughts and thus, it was a form of prayer. What I didn't know was that I missed out on many of God's blessings because I had not actually addressed Him or figuratively walked into His presence. If I'm only thinking about God, He cannot respond to me. My thoughts had conceived of Him and my plans had included Him, but like the silent spouse in a marriage, there was no real conversation.

To overcome our unwillingness to obey God, we need to pray and ask Jesus for deliverance. We should be so bathed in prayer that we can discern the voice of Jesus Christ. God must remove the veil from our minds that allows deception. And here is the greatest deception: that somehow there are life-fulfilling avenues other than Jesus Christ.

Eventually, our distraction with this world will end. Once we come to terms with this truth, carnal Christianity is easier to leave behind. May that not be on our deathbed! Deliverance comes from God when we pray for it and believe He is able to give it to us. It almost sounds like a cop-out to rely on God to give us the desire to obey Him fully. But in this area, we simply cannot pull ourselves up by our own bootstraps.

More prayer can never hurt us. More prayer will give us an inner discernment that will show us right from wrong. More prayer will begin to form a barrier within us toward sinful behavior. More prayer will bring help from heaven into our living rooms. Days and weeks go by and we refuse to spend time with God in what should be the highest joy imaginable. Let us resolve to spend time with God in prayer that we may obey His slightest command easily and with joy. Then, help from heaven will flow to us in new and unbounded ways!

Let us pray: *Dear Jesus, please deliver me from the sin of prayerlessness. Fill my heart with the joy of Your song. Let me speak with You throughout the day and contemplate Your majesty and glory. May Your presence fill me to overflowing. I pray for the desire to pray and for the desire to obey You fully. I thank You and praise You, and it is in Your name that I pray. Amen.*

Our Whole Hearts

John Calvin wrote, "For, until men feel that they owe everything to God, that they are cherished by his paternal care, and that he is the author of all their blessings, so that naught is to be looked for away from him, they will never submit to him in voluntary obedience; nay, unless they place their entire happiness in him, they will never yield up their whole selves to him in truth and sincerity." Calvin also said that "Not a particle of light, or wisdom, or justice, or power, or rectitude, or genuine truth, will anywhere be found, which does not flow from Him, and of which He is not the cause."[7]

If we really think about it, God owns everything. Most of us have been guilty of pursing worldly ventures with our whole hearts much more than we have pursued God because we did not attribute all we have or ever will have to God alone. I don't know about you, but a question I've had to ask myself is this: "Why must I try every other source before seeking God for all of my desires?" Do I have to prove to myself that there is no other source but God? The lie of the devil is that there are other sources of supply, happiness, and blessing; I just haven't tried hard enough or given them enough time or resources. If God is to answer my prayers for help from heaven, He is obliged to make these other indirect sources fail in order to show me He is the direct Source of all that is.

"You will seek me and find me when you seek me with all your heart" (Jer 29:13). Whole-hearted pursuit of God is required for anyone who is serious about finding Him. "But when he asks, he must believe and not doubt, because he who doubts is like a wave of the sea, blown and tossed by the wind. That man should not think he will receive anything from the Lord; he is a double-minded man, unstable in all

---

[7] Source: John Calvin, *Institutes of the Christian Religion* (Originally published in 1536, republished by Christian Classics Ethereal Library, Grand Rapids, MI) p. 47.

he does" (Jas 1:6-8). Being double-minded is not like having a disease such as attention deficit disorder (ADD). Instead, God considers it a moral flaw. I would lump carnal Christianity, double-mindedness, and half-heartedness together. These are all products of the same flaw – an inability to wholeheartedly seek the Lord.

Although we have failed in the past, let us now trust God directly to provide a clear path for wholehearted commitment to Him. Let us give Jesus all of our fears about trusting God completely. Let's believe that God can take care of all those external pressures so we can give Him complete, whole-hearted obedience.

Let us pray: *Lord Jesus, I ask You to grant me the blessing of whole-hearted obedience to You. Show me the futility of fleshly pursuits. Close down the idea in my mind that there are rewards for me apart from You. Please replace all of my independent willfulness with a desire to obey You completely. Direct my joy-sensing radar to You and You alone. I ask this in Your name, Amen.*

Loving God Wholeheartedly

We are commanded to love the Lord our God with all our heart and with all our soul and with all our mind and with all our strength (Mk 12:30). But what if we don't really love God? How do we make ourselves love Him if we don't? The simple answer is, we can't. The Bible says we cannot come to Jesus unless God draws us to Him. So if we desire to love God but don't know what that is like, we must ask God to grant us the experience of loving Him as a gift.

Because God first loved us, we are free to experience His love *before* loving Him back. The apostle Paul knew this was the key to finding a whole-hearted love of Christ. "And I pray that you, being rooted and established in love, may have power, together with all the saints, to grasp how wide and long and high and deep is the love of Christ, and to know this love that surpasses knowledge - that you may be filled to the measure of all the fullness of God" (Eph 3:17b-19). To truly understand the full depth of love Christ has for us, we need the experience of being flooded and filled with God Himself. God is love and being filled with Him fills us with love.

109

When we wholeheartedly surrender to Christ and receive His love, there is a secret to keeping that love flowing into our hearts. It involves sharing this love. Jesus commanded us to share His love with one another. St. John tells us that if we don't love our fellow believers who we have seen, we can't love God who we haven't seen (1 Jn 4:20). You and I have the power to withhold love from people. And because we reap what we sow, if we withhold love from other people that we are commanded to love, it automatically stops our flow of love from heaven.

When Jesus commanded us to love one another, He knew that sharing love is a mechanism that releases the flow of God's love into our souls. It doesn't matter if those around us deserve our love or return it. If we want the love of the Holy Spirit to be magnified in our own hearts, we must share this unlimited gift with others. It's not a zero-sum game! God is the source of this love, so we don't have to worry about getting it from other people or running out of it. Love is the highest form of spiritual warfare. We need to dedicate ourselves to living a life of love. We need to study it, learn it, seek it, give it, and cherish it. We cannot exhaust its potential and we will never tire of this quest. The essence of true help from heaven is the living love of Christ!

Let us pray: *Dear Jesus, I know I have not always loved others as I should. I am ashamed that I have not loved You as I should. I want to love You and obey Your commands. I repent from selfishness and a refusal to share Your love. I ask for Your forgiveness. Dear Lord, please fill me with Yourself and give me the power obey You and to love others today. May I reflect Your glorious love to all fellow believers and even to those who may despise me. Amen.*

Part 8 - Implementing the Answer

One Final Caveat

Help from heaven cannot be reduced to a series of formulas. American Christians are very pragmatic. We find out what works, and then we do that. We want to know that if you do X, Y, and Z, you will have good results. We are "working" our Christianity to get things from heaven. Depending upon our attitudes, this can reduce to practical magic. The idea that if I have enough faith, I can use God to move mountains is not what Jesus meant when He chastised His believers for having too little faith. I cannot cause God to do anything. If God moves in my behalf, it is only because of His love for Jesus Christ that is credited to me.

Much of American evangelism takes the position that sin is bad and because of it, one must make a decision to follow Christ. Once that decision has been made, it is up to the person to quit sinning and think instead, "What Would Jesus Do?" These Christians must keep themselves clean and think wholesome thoughts so they live up to the measure of Jesus Christ. By doing good, they gain points with God so that He hears their prayers for assistance. Perhaps 90 percent of American Christians think this way.

I'm sorry, but there is something missing. So much of this is a mechanical process of following formulas in order to gain results. Witch doctors and shamans do the same thing. Let me ask, where is the reverential fear and love of God in all of this? What life-altering process is involved if I simply decide one day to try to follow Jesus instead of actually surrendering my whole being to Him and letting Him run my life from the inside? If I keep my personality intact and add Christ, my Christianity is as weak as I am. But if Jesus has command and I do Christianity in His strength, God's kingdom advances on earth as it is in heaven.

Our only hope for help from heaven is to believe that our power with God comes through Jesus Christ and His atoning grace. Our job is not to try to imitate Jesus, but instead, to let Jesus Himself operate through us when we are born again in His Spirit. Our faith is a gift of God. We can't believe what we can't believe. But with God Himself living inside us, we can believe in all the promises that He gave us in the Bible.

How We Change Our Lives

Do not fall into the trap of thinking information, of itself, will change you and somehow open the windows of heaven. Only God can change us on the inside by His Holy Spirit. Information and education is good, but it cannot change the future of America for the better unless people use it to honor and glorify God. We spend more than three quarters of a trillion dollars each year on education as if it will cure what ails America. But it will not. Technology is not the answer. Simply reading this book will not change your life. The only thing that reverses our course toward destruction is surrendering our hearts and lives to God for real.

Are you tired of going through the motions? Is it time to get real with God? Romans 12:2 says, "Do not conform any longer to the pattern of this world, but be transformed by the renewing of your mind." A renewed mind is not the product of education. It results from God's touch. Romans 12:1 talks about how we are touched by God through our worship: "Therefore, I urge you, brothers, in view of God's mercy, to offer your bodies as living sacrifices, holy and pleasing to God—this is your spiritual act of worship." We cannot be smug about offering our bodies as living sacrifices to God. We cannot be detached from it. A living sacrifice to God is one that enters God's holy presence without any defense or agenda.

Many of us Bible believers quote doctrine in order to preserve the coldness of our hearts. We make Christianity into a theology so we don't have to offer our bodies as living sacrifices. If Christianity is solely an intellectual pursuit, our hearts are free to be cold and detached. No. As I read on in Romans 12, I see what the apostle Paul was getting at: "Love must be sincere. Hate what is evil; cling to what is good. Be devoted to one another in brotherly love. Honor one another above yourselves. Never be lacking in zeal, but keep your spiritual fervor, serving the Lord. Be joyful in hope, patient in affliction, faithful in prayer" (Rom 12:9-12). Paul finishes with this admonition: "Do not be overcome by evil, but overcome evil with good" (Rom 12:21). None of this involves education or giving people new information. It involves overcoming the evil in our own hearts by asking Jesus to change us by His power and love.

Arguing and debating will not change a person's mind. Instead, it often fuels their research into better arguments. To change people's minds, their hearts must first be changed. This happens when the love of Jesus becomes the focal point and melts their cold hearts.

Let us pray: *Lord Jesus, I want You to rule my heart. Please do what is necessary to make that happen. I pray for America and I pray for the world at large. May all people everywhere come to know You before the dark times. Lord Jesus, may we experience Your love as the greatest inducement to serve You. Amen.*

Expand Your Territory

Several years ago, a small book was published called *The Prayer of Jabez.* It was a best seller because believers who read it learned how to pray for abundance and have their prayers answered. For non-believers, it was popular because it seemed like an incantation that would bring prosperity. The prayer itself goes like this: "Jabez cried out to the God of Israel, 'Oh, that you would bless me and enlarge my territory! Let your hand be with me, and keep me from harm so that I will be free from pain.' And God granted his request" (1 Chr 4:10). "Enlarge my territory!" If we are thinking the way God is thinking, that is the prayer of a person in ministry who wants to reach more and more people with the Gospel of Jesus Christ.

You may have seen football teams use a "prevent" defense to hang on to a lead at the end of the game. Often, the desire not to lose is an invitation for the other team to take the initiative and score and win. Jesus is telling us His Gospel is not defensive in nature. Jesus said that the gates of hell would not prevail against His church. Gates are a defensive structure. The Good News of the Gospel can tear down walls and heal those who are captives to brokenness.

It turns out that the new plan of spreading the Gospel or "good news" is the same as the original plan laid down by Jesus Himself. Our attitude has to be one of spreading the Word rather than getting it and retreating into our churches to wait for the end. We must have a strong offense and not worry about a defensive posture. It doesn't matter that some people dislike our message. God has prepared the hearts of other people who need to hear what you have to say.

All you have to do is tell your story. How did you meet Jesus? What was it like? People are literally dying to know! You may be the only one that will give them the good news of Jesus Christ in a personal way they can actually relate to and use in their own lives. We need to expand our territory by sharing the help from heaven we have received!

Another way to enlarge our territory is to give to the Lord for His work and share the Gospel with others. God multiplies the return on our investment in the Gospel. The subtitle of this book comes from one of my favorite promises in the Bible about help from heaven: "'Bring all the tithes into the storehouse, that there may be food in my house, and try me now in this,' says the LORD of hosts, 'If I will not open for you the windows of heaven and pour out for you such blessing that there will not be room enough to receive it'" (Mal 3:10 NKJV). God is asking you and me to test Him in this promise by giving money to His work. He will open the floodgates of heaven and pour out so much blessing that we cannot contain it. Do you want this type of help from heaven? I certainly do.

Let us pray: *Lord Jesus, I pray for a generous heart to share my resources with others. May I do this in the spirit of winning souls to Your kingdom.*

I want to take You up on Your promise of return for my tithe. I trust You with all that I have. Amen.

Leap of Faith

A leap of faith is not a choice between rationality and irrationality. It is not a blind leap. It is a deliberate surrender of control of our lives to God, based on sound evidence and rational thought. Jesus said we are to "lose" our lives for Him in order to gain them. But there is profound fear in actually handing over our lives to Christ. It is similar to the choice of staying in the seventh floor window of a burning building, or jumping into the net held by the firemen below. Survival depends on making that jump, but fear grips us when we actually have to do it. Some people freeze and can't let go.

In America, political correctness brings fear to Christians, because we don't want to be disliked. Many Christians would like to stand up for the principles in the Bible concerning abortion, homosexuality, or the exclusive claims of Jesus Christ. But fear of reprisals and being branded as radicals, bigots, or homophobes has pushed these Christians into silence. They choose not to act on their religious convictions. In a certain sense, this is cowardice.

When we are afraid to do what is right, we reach the decision point arranged by God. God wants us to confront our fears about following Him. We are to "do it afraid" as Joyce Meyer has said. The fear of persecution is simply the fear of leaving what we think is a safe place. It is about giving up control and trusting God. This is what every Christian must face. We must lose our lives in order to save them. But when we do, we understand from experience, that God is bigger than life, that we are temporary sojourners on the earth, and that the defense of our "preciousness" was never really ours to defend in the first place. It belongs to God.

So I urge you to take that leap of faith. Confront the fear of losing control over your life and give it up to God. If you stay awake during that experience (some people close their eyes when they jump), you will know God in a totally different light. As someone who has taken the leap, I can assure you that God is there, that He will catch you, and that you can trust Him.

Let us pray: *Lord Jesus, please give me the courage to take the leap of faith that You have designed just for me. I realize that others may have a different fear to overcome. But You are sufficient for each of us. Thank You for Your abiding presence now and forever. Amen.*

Receiving Help from Heaven

Every one of us has received help from heaven. After reading this book, you may have a new perspective on opening the windows of heaven and filling yourself with its holy bounty. As you know by now, I believe the true help from heaven is God Himself. The only thing He can really give us is more of Himself. When we are filled with His Holy Spirit, we are filled with life itself. So we must remember that in the end, this life is not about us. God's purpose in us is to glorify Himself. Thus, our purpose in receiving help from heaven should be to receive the King of Glory within the temple of our body and honor Him with our whole being. That is our calling. That is our reward.

The secret of enjoying help from heaven is to become a conduit of praise for heaven's King. Every ounce of rebellion will need to be surrendered to Jesus. If you feel uncomfortable with any aspect of the sovereignty of God in your life, you will need to prayerfully hand it over to Him. If any description of God in the Bible is offensive to you, think about the sensibilities that are being trampled and then intentionally trample them yourself. Those feelings of offense are the vestiges of our rebellion against God.

In heaven, there is a holy refrain that echoes 24/7: "The twenty-four elders fall down before him who sits on the throne, and worship him who lives forever and ever. They lay their crowns before the throne and say: 'You are worthy, our Lord and God, to receive glory and honor and power, for you created all things, and by your will they were created and have their being'" (Rv 4:10-11).

We too can join this heavenly chorus of praise and worship. That is our election, selected by Jesus before the foundation of the world (Eph 1:4). He is our direct connection to God the Father (Jn 14:6). Therefore, as you enter into His presence, let the love of Jesus penetrate every aspect of your life. There is no downside to this. True help from heaven is having a living Savior reside in your heart now and forever. Receive the *fullness* of Jesus Christ today!

Let us pray: *Lord Jesus Christ, I thank You for Your help from heaven. May I grow each day in the intimate knowledge of You and Your Holy Spirit. May Your living love radiate within my heart. Teach me to wait in Your presence and absorb Your radiant love. May this love move me to do great things within my circle of influence. I pray that everyone everywhere come to know You and the power of Your love. I thank You, Jesus, and pray this to Your glory, Amen.*

Printed in the United States
By Bookmasters